Twelve Years In Care

By
Alam Navsa

Copyright©AlamNavsa2020

Rev.iv

Table of Contents

Chapter 1.....The Beginning
Chapter 2.....First Accident
Chapter 3.....Bee Sting
Chapter 4.....Little Criminals
Chapter 5.....The Wicked Witch
Chapter 6.....First Move
Chapter 7.....Eversley Children's Home
Chapter 8.....New Friends
Chapter 9.....Karma
Chapter 10....First Holiday
Chapter 11....Second Name Change
Chapter 12....Christmas Angel
Chapter 13....Barbara's Revenge
Chapter 14....Hot Summer
Chapter 15....Humiliation
Chapter 16....Old Fool
Chapter 17....Hospital Visit
Chapter 18....Summer Horror
Chapter 19....Second Foster
Chapter 20....Fire Incident
Chapter 21....Too Young to Shave
Chapter 22....Red House
Chapter 23....Close Encounter
Chapter 24....Musselburgh Harbour
Chapter 25....Butlins
Chapter 26....The Grove
Chapter 27....Burgh Primary School
Chapter 28....Christmas Home
Chapter 29....Mrs Colins
Chapter 30....RAF Leuchars
Chapter 31....Near Drowning
Chapter 32....Runaway
Chapter 33....New Dog
Chapter 34....Boy And A Chisel
Chapter 35....A Night Back To Eversley
Chapter 36....A Bloody Finger
Chapter 37....Lonely Old Man
Chapter 38....First Family Contact
Chapter 39....Floating Rock
Chapter 40....School Plant
Chapter 41....Nightmare Ends
Chapter 42....Headmaster's Office
Chapter 43....Mrs Mop
Chapter 44....Pantomime And Dares
Chapter 45....Departure

Introduction
Contains violence and strong language.

This story is based on my life growing up in three Children's Homes and two Foster Care homes over a twelve-year period from the age of seven weeks.

The characters in the book are based on real people. Some names have been changed in some part to protect their true identity. The book is designed to give an insight into what life was like for many children like myself who found themselves in similar situations from a period between 1965 to 1977, in most cases through a social care system in which some cared not for what they were employed to do, but an opportunity to bully, beat and in worse cases, sexually abuse those in their charge.

Sexual abuse was rampant in homes across the country. I was close to being sexually abused twice throughout those twelve years, but survived on both occasions. That said, I was not immune to other abuses that took place, readers will have to judge for themselves what they regard as sexual, physical, and mental abuse. That does not mean I wasn't sexually abused. This book only covers the first 12 years.

This book gives secrets of which I have never revealed. I've kept these secrets more through a personal feeling of guilt, anger, and shame. It was in 2015, when I started this book after meeting a young person on a camping trip, who seemed more than happy to talk about his experiences at home before being taking into protected care. It's his ordeal, and ability to talk openly about his experience, that has giving me the courage to reveal my own life and start writing this book.

This book gives graphic details of beatings and humiliation. Physical punishments in many homes were beyond what would be considered corporal punishment, yet at they time may never have been regarded as abuse. And there's a distinct difference between what's considered Corporal Punishment, and what's considered physical abuse.

Children's homes were designed to protect Children from harm, abuse, and difficulties within family environments. In many instances some of these homes violated these protections. some with senior level knowledge, some without. In most cases, Children were protected by their carers and went on to live normal lives. Many who were abused to this day still struggle with the traumatic experience they suffered. But equally many push it to the back of their minds trying to move forward. But it's not easy. Certain things can trigger these memories off, such as tv programs, news reports, or just people talking about it.

I've been asked by many people what life was like in homes. It's never been easy to sit with someone and talk about it, so I wrote this book not solely to show the negative side of home life, but home life in general from the above, to the fun and crazy moments over that period. Every child who's lived in a home has their own story. Some good, some bad. This is mine. I hope this book will help readers understand that we were just normal kids brought up in circumstances not of our doing, and grew up to live normal adult lives.

Chapter 1
The Beginning

It's February 8th, 1965. A new-born boy takes his first breath off air in this world. His birth is normal with no complications.

He's born in Stepney, London, to Mary, a Scottish mother of three girls and now one boy. Born or even conceived after her separation from his Father of Indian origins, and who has custody of two of his older sisters. His mother bore a child prior to her marriage. She will become a vital part of his final stages in the last year of the home where he resides. He is christened Alan Derek Navsa, mixed race with blue eyes.

He's moved up to Glasgow within weeks of his birth. Within a short period of time he ends up in a children's home at seven weeks old. It has never been clear as to what had lead him to being in the home. His dad was never consistent in his reasons changing aspects of his explanation every time he told him. His dad told him many years later that he was put there by social services because they felt he was too young to travel to England where they were moving. Though later he himself contradicts that version when he tells him he would regularly visit him when he was a bus conductor between Glasgow and Helensburgh. That again did not add up, as the distance between Helensburgh and Rhu is three miles, which would make it impossible for him to get between the two and back in that time scale. The other inconsistency is his claim that he was paying for his upkeep during his time in the children's homes. They were state run homes, not private run, which meant he couldn't have paid. And his last claim that he spent his life trying to find him but couldn't. The documents claim that social workers tracked him down, and no attempt over the twelve years were made to locate him, or even reclaim him.

Alan Derek is taken to a home on the north west side of the river Clyde, a small up-market town by the name of Rhu. The building itself is a large gothic style 18th century mansion known as Blairvadach children's home that sits inside the mouth of Gare Loch. There is a clear view of the mouth of the Clyde from the hillside where the building sits. Set in beautiful surrounding with hills leading from the rear, though mostly hidden by the tall trees surrounding most of the perimeter.

Seven weeks old is the time he is placed in this home. For years he had no idea why he was there. Who put him there. Whether or not he had a family. Are they alive. Are they dead. Did they want him. Is he abandoned. Or did he do anything to make them dislike him. These are the kind of thoughts that will haunt him for the next 11 years as he begins to understand his surroundings and his life.

Alan Derek first becomes more alert as he begins to walk. It's in the porta cabin that sits on the front lawn, in front of the main building where he takes his first steps, as he grabs on to the part dividing wall that separates the playroom from the dining room. He draws himself to reach the bannister at the top of the half dividing wall and stands on his two feet taking his first few steps. And after a few falls from this repeated process, he finds he can walk like the other giants around him.

The next four years will be of mixed emotions unsure of

what his life is about, but it's the only life he has at this time. Surrounded by other boys and girls, some his age, some younger, some older. His world is a cocoon. He spends little time outdoors, particularly through winter. Most of their time is spent between the playroom in the porta cabin, and the playroom adjacent to the main house, which is an extended part of the main building. At times they are allowed to go outside, and in doing so makes the most of it.

It is dry and clear, but not too cold. The kids are out in the backyard, just running around, playing, and shouting as kids do. The older kids can be heard but not seen, as they are playing round the frontside of the home. Alan Derek is playing on top of the small hill just beyond the yard with a few others when a voice shouts for them to come indoors just as the big orange light begins to fall off the other end of the world behind the trees, as seen through the young three-year-old eyes which he was finding fascinating whilst distracted and is the last to heed the call to go indoors. As he approaches the door, the sound of a piercing and deafening sound rings out. It's the first time he's ever heard such a noise and it's loud, so loud he fears for his life and runs back up the little hill that overlooks the house as the remaining light is fading away. He's panicking, crying, terrified, and doesn't know where to turn or go until one of the staff members Joyce, either heard or saw him and comes to his aid.

"are you ok".

she asks as she tries to comfort him. But his heart is still racing.

"the noise, loud noise"

as he tries to describe what happened. Of course, the noise had already stopped before she came to his rescue. She takes his tiny hand, and says,

"come on, I'll take you in",

but as they walk back towards the door, the piercing sound rings out again. He pulls his hand away from her loose grip running back up the hill screaming. She follows reassuring him.

"its ok, its just the telephone",

But he's never seen or heard a telephone and looks bewildered as Joyce tries to explain what a telephone is. Every word she's saying to him is just going over his head as he has no idea what she's talking about. The noise has again stopped, and Joyce takes his hand again walking him back. As they get through the door, Joyce points to the bell on the wall that is the culprit of his torture, and the telephone through the open door of a dark room lit by the light from the corridor they are walking through.

"there, you see, that's all it is, nothing to be frightened of",

but as luck would not have it, the bell rings out again as they pass it. This time he is inside and runs like hell to get away from the sound straight into the only room he's familiar with, the playroom. Even though it's dark and empty, he feels safe. He's developed a phobia for bells and loud unfamiliar sounds, which is a result of the extensions used to increase the volume of the telephone as the place is so big. The high pitch of the ringing tone is such, it becomes annoying to his ears.

He sits on the benches and paces himself side to side all alone in the dark playroom, too small to reach the light switch until he's sure the sound has stopped for good. He peeps out the door regularly wondering if he should risk it. Eventually Joyce walks in.

"here you are, we've been looking all over for you".

she says pausing for a bit just looking at him.

"come on, it's bedtime".

she says while taking his hand and leaving the room. They walk through the hall passing the bell as Alan Derek stares at it hoping it doesn't ring again. Up the wide stairs to the first door on the right at the top of the stairs, and along a corridor leading to his bedroom. The door handle is round made with glass and set on a glass flowery designed plate. Joyce opens the huge six panelled door and they walk in to a large room mostly filled with cots and a few high single metal framed beds. The bed furthest to the window is where Alan Derek sleeps. The room is large with a single sash window on the end near Alan Dereks bed. The large side walls where the beds and cots line up, are decorated with period style mouldings around the door and window frames. The ceiling is decorated with moulded covings and a circular decorative moulding in the middle, with a black ceiling rose at the base, with a long twisted black wire leading to a black pendant light. Joyce helps him to undress and change into his pyjamas. Then he climbs into bed already warm from the heating being constantly on allowing him to sleep with comfort. Occasionally he's woken up by the babies cries as the nights go on. As a toddler you don't understand seasons. But the one thing that stands out for the young minds learning they're surroundings is the time of year. When it's hotter, the bedroom curtains are closed. But when it's colder, the bedroom curtains are occasionally left open, as during winter it's dark enough not to need the curtains closed, and with no other buildings around, they have all the privacy they need.

Chapter 2
The first accident

The Days are longer and hotter. The older kids are at school with just the toddlers left in the Playroom. The door leading to the yard from the playroom is unusually open and the kids are playing both inside and out. A wooden climbing frame is erected in the playroom and most of the toys are outside in the yard. Alan Derek goes outside to the sight of tricycles and scooters in all shapes and sizes. One tricycle catches his eye. A two-seater tricycle which seems to be the most popular item in the yard with a queue waiting to try it out. Two at a time sit on this contraption with each child wanting to steer, and Alan Derek is no different waiting his turn. He doesn't have to wait long and is lucky enough to steer on his first ride. One circuit in the yard is what they're allowed. He can't complain as it is a large yard, and by the time he gets back to the starting point, he's already shattered despite the tricycle having two sets of peddles for each rider. After having a long five second rest, he's off to another ride. This time a three-wheeler scooter. He stands on it searching for the seat and peddles. There's none to be seen. He's confused and looks at the staff. Joyce and Margaret are already laughing realising what he's doing, though he hasn't clocked on he's the joke. Not one to give up, he continues trying to figure out how to get this complex contraption on three wheels with handlebars to work. He's distracted by Joyce walking over to him asking,

"are you stuck".

"no" he replies.

pausing slightly then adding

"it doesn't move",

"you push with your foot" she says,

"oh"

he replies as he puts both feet on the ground and starts walking and pushing it by the handlebars causing a roar of laughter from the staff.

"No" she says, whilst still laughing,

"not like that," pausing as she tries to console herself,

"put one foot on the plate, and push with the other along the ground",

Alan Derek pauses for a bit to try and figure out the mathematics of this, saying,

"ahh, ok"

following her instructions and pushing with one foot with the other on the plate. But as the speed builds up he suddenly realises he isn't going to stop. He looks back at Joyce hoping for some instructions, then looks forward quickly realising he's running out of tarmac. Then suddenly he flies over the handlebars as he hits the grass verge as the vehicle comes to a sudden stop. There's silence for a moment then movement. Alan Derek lifts his head as blood pours from his nose. Joyce seeing this immediately reacts racing over to him and moving the scooter which is partially laying over him.

"put your head up".

she says as she pinches the top of his nose. He's trying to be brave, but the tears are telling. He gets distracted by the strange sound he keeps hearing coming from behind him which he can't see because of the Trees that separates the home from the outside world. A sound he hears almost daily but not as annoying as the bell. To him it just feels strange because he can't see what's causing it.

"let's get you on your feet".

Joyce says as she continues to hold his nose. Up he gets with Joyce placing her hand on his back and walking him into the house via the playroom doors. She continues to hold his nose taking the longer route when it would be quicker to go through the other door where the toilets are. Alan Derek is thinking she was trying to avoid a repeat of the time when the phone rang. She takes him into the washroom running cold water over his nose then cleaning him up.

"We need to get you out of those bloodstained clothes" she says,

with Alan Derek looking down at the blood covering the front of his shirt. Joyce takes him upstairs to his room and takes his top off leaving him in just his vest whilst she looks for another shirt. He sits on his bed waiting. Soon after Joyce returns with a clean folded shirt and puts it on him. Alan Derek is still teared up, not because of the bloody nose, but because he hurt his knee as he fell to the ground.

Joyce takes him over to the window next to his bed and opens it.

"look down there" she says,

The window sill is deep because of the huge stone walls, so Alan Derek has to stretch himself over the sill to see what's below. His window just happens to be right above the door that leads to the bell that tortured him before. But she was showing him a strange motionless creature like a huge slug, that lay in front of the door. Alan Derek has no idea what it is. It could have been a Dog, or a Cat. For him it's all new, the only living things he ever sees are the other humans and birds, he's never seen a cat or a dog, so this creature is exactly what it is to him, a creature. Could that have been the reason she took him through the playroom. He never did find out what it was, but it did calm him down.

That night, Joyce does her usual routine of changing him. As she takes his trousers down she looks up at him and asks.

"what happened there".

Alan Derek looks down at the injury on his knee which is partially covered in dry blood.

"I fell off the scooter" he replies,

"why didn't you say anything" Joyce asks,

"I did" he said, though not quite sure if he did.

Joyce leaves the room returning after a few minutes with a kidney dish and cleans his wound before helping him with his pyjamas and putting him into bed.

That same year, but just another day. The door in the playroom to the yard is used more since the incident with the strange creature, and with it being hot allows a breeze to flow through the playroom. Most of the other toddlers are outside, with only a few remaining inside including Alan Derek as it's too hot in the afternoon sun, and he's not keen on that strange sound he keeps hearing coming from beyond the trees. Late afternoon everyone is coming back into the playroom. The doors are closed and then a shout comes from Margaret.

"WHO DID THIS"

everybody stops what they're doing and looks over to Margaret.

"WHO DID THIS I SAID".

pointing to a puddle of urine on the floor not that far from where Alan Derek is playing.

"WAS IT YOU" looking directly at Alan Derek.

"no" he replies,

"YOU'RE THE ONE CLOSEST TO IT" she says,

Then speed walks over to him, grabbing him from under his arms, then lifting him thrusting his legs forward and placing him over the urine with the seat of his trousers sliding him from side to side mopping the urine up, leaving the seat of his behind soaked despite his repeated cries of denial.

"You can stay in them for the rest of the day. Now get over to that corner, and don't move".

she says as she begins to calm down despite his continued denials. He's hoping Joyce would come to his aid, but she is no where to be seen that day. It seems she has her day off. No one likes Margret. She is evil, and always shouting and hitting the kids mostly for no reason. And It's like she enjoys doing it.

Chapter 3
The Bee Sting

Summer is in full swing. The older kids are off school for the Summer holidays. It's hot, and most of the younger residents are topless including Alan Derek. The older kids will be using the yard and the main Playroom, so the younger children will be using the porta cabin throughout the holidays.

"Get into pairs".

Margaret orders the younger children gathered in the main entrance which is split into two sections by two huge part wood carved, part stone wall, with the main stairwell in the second part, as she pushes some of them to partner up.

"hold hands" she continues,

then moments later a slap is heard from behind Alan Derek as she says,

"that means you too Archie".

who's now rubbing his face where her hand connected. They walk through one door that leads them to a smaller entrance hall, leading to a few wide wall to wall stairs, walking down then out through a large front door taking them outside, then down a few more steps before they make their way down the winding track. As they do, a sudden scream from Alan Derek is heard as he is stung by a wasp on his bare shoulder. His shoulder almost immediately swells up on the area where he's stung. Still scream-

ing in pain, a woman's head appears f
dow shouting,

"WHATS GOING ON".

"HES BEEN STUNG" Joyce shouts ba

"BRING HIM UP" the woman shouts.

With that, Joyce takes him from the line, taking him back into the building then upstairs to what looks like an office where he is treated for the sting, later rejoining his friends at the porta cabin.

As the hot days ware on, the kids spend most of their summer on the front lawn in view of the building site where buildings are being demolished across the road. The demolition site seems to be some kind of old industrial complex. Possibly an old shipping yard, or steel works. The home received some form of notification explaining that the tower on the site is going to be demolished by explosives, and the garden needs to be cleared for safety. On the day of the demolition, the kids are walked down to the Porta cabin. They're shuffled in and Margret tells them.

"there's going to be an explosion, and the tower over there will fall. If you want to see it, you can watch it from the windows",

they fill all the rooms. The play area, dining room and the meeting room, covering every window. One of the workers is by the gates to the front garden. Margret waves to him and he gave a thumbs up to signal everything is safe. The kids are told to count down from ten after they hear a horn.

ediately the horn goes off. Everyone is counting with Margret leading as none of them have the to count up, let alone count down. As soon as they zero nothing happens. Just as the kids are about to turn away, a sudden burst of dust appears in the distance followed by the sound of the explosion as the tower falls to the ground. Two days later, they're invited to visit the demolition site.

Early evening after work stops, there's silence from the demolition site as the bulldozers and diggers are left where they pushed and dug. The kids from the home are escorted to the site just across the road from the main gates. For Alan Derek, this is his first experience on the other side of the homes compound in his three years at the home. As they enter the site, the grassless ground bares the tracks indented by the chain tracks of the bulldozers and tractors that were a constant noise pollution to the home. They're taken up closely to the machines that look like small matchbox vehicles from the lawn of the home where the kids often watch from. But up close, they look like monsters causing some of the young visitors to freak out. The buckets at the front look like huge dinosaurs as they walk from one monster to the other. The bulldozers are the most popular amongst the young minds for its sheer size and looks. For days after the visit, the toy tractor was always fought over by almost all the kids to mimic the huge bulldozer that captured their young minds.

The end of the summer holidays are only a few days away. The younger kids are spending their last few days in the porta cabin. Alan Derek is not feeling well on this particular day and spends most of the day inside the Porta cabin playing in the playing area on his own whilst the others play outside. At some point the doorbell rings out. Alan Derek still with his fear of bells, runs and takes cover under the dining table in the dining room adjacent to the playroom where he was playing. It rings out again and Joyce comes out from the kitchen, walks over to the door to opens it. As she returns, she stops by the table and says.

"you can come out now".

Joyce already aware of his fears calms him down and takes him to the door showing him the bell situated above the door explaining to him how it works. She opens the door and points out the push button to him, a small black rectangular box with a white round button in the centre.

"When someone comes to the door, they press that button to tell you they are there" she says,

"go on, press the button" she tells him,

Alan Derek slowly takes his finger to the button. Touching it but not pressing it,

"go on, don't be scared" Joyce says patiently,

She's not pushing him, but his heart is racing. He presses the button and as soon as it rings, he lets it go. With Joyce by his side he feels safe.

"Go on, try it again".

he follows her instructions and presses it again, and again it rings out.

"see, it's nothing, just a bell".

He presses it again longer this time, a smile appears on his face,

"ok" Joyce says,

"That's enough".

she adds as he begins to get overconfident.

"let's go back in".

With that his fears of bells disappear.

Chapter 4
Little Criminals

Summer holidays have ended and the older children have restarted school along with some of those who spent most of the Summer with the younger kids. There's only seven remaining and now back in the main playroom. They watch as the school children walk past the playroom windows in their black uniforms making their way to school.

"When do we get to go" Archie asks Margret,

"you've still got another year Archie" Margret replies.

"And me" asks Alan Derek,

"you have another year too" she replies.

"Right, I have to leave the room for a couple of minutes, so you better be on your best behaviour whilst I'm gone, ok?"

Margret says as she walks towards to door not waiting for a reply. She opens the door and walks out shutting it as she goes causing an echo surrounding the almost empty room as it slams shut. There are no toys, and the climbing frame has been taken down with the seven kids just stuck doing nothing. No one knows where the toys are kept, but two boxes are seen on top of the shelf above the door at the front of the room.

"How do we get the toys down" Archie asks,

everyone is looking at each other,

"you're the biggest".

Archie says to Alan Derek in reference to his height.

"How do I get up, it's high"

Alan Derek asks as they all look up to the shelf with him being less than half the height. He climbs on to the bench by the window, climbing on to the ledge of the window. With the top window slightly ajar, he pulls himself up placing his foot on the middle frame of the window giving him just enough reach to grab the shelf. It isn't enough though. He pushes himself up using the open window to support his foot, then on to the shelf crawling along it to reach the two boxes. He pushes them down one by one, then gets down in the reverse of how he got up. As they open the boxes they find they're full of women's clothes, high heal shoes, dresses, and other bits. Of the seven children left none are girls, so the boys just simply pass time walking and falling around in the shoes. Some in high heels laughing as others hold up the bras. Not long after the door suddenly opens and both Margaret and Joyce walk in. Margaret is clearly not amused though Joyce is. She looks at the kids then looks up to the shelf trying to figure out how the boxes ended up on the floor. She obviously thought there's no way they could have climbed onto that shelf, and there is no other way they would have got the boxes down.

"Get them off and put them back in the box".

Margaret says with an angry tone still trying to figure out how they ended up on the floor. She tells Joyce to get the toys out. The kids are watching closely to where she goes as she walks over to the bench box and opens it. It never crossed Alan Derek's mind that his climb was a total waste of time as he and his fellow partners in crime run over to the toy box.

The nights are getting darker and the younger kids are no longer spending much time outside. Most of their days are now spent in the main playroom. It's late afternoon and the kids are getting bored and rowdy. The staff are beginning to get frustrated at the noise, particularly Margret, who's known for her short temper and loose hand when it comes to slapping kids around. Joyce leaves the room to do other duties.

"SHUTUP AND SIT ON THE BENCH"

Margaret shouts just after Joyce leaves. The benches are built into the wall on both sides and fixed to the floor.

"AND SIT QUIETLY OR YOU'LL FEEL THE BACK OF MY HAND"

she adds. With that the kids huddle together on the bench. Margaret looks at them, her eyes almost popping out

"SEPARATE YOURSELVES" ranting on,

"ONE OF YOU IN EACH CORNER, AND THE REST OF YOU SPREAD APART IN THE MIDDLE ON BOTH SIDES".

No one dares argue. Alan Derek is on the far end close to the door that leads to the yard. Archie is on the opposite side in the middle. Archie and Alan Derek get on well together, they look at each other. Alan Derek gives Archie a smirk trying not to be noticed or make it obvious. Archie a ginger head boy of the same age smirks back. This is boring for anyone let alone the young kids. They try and make excuses to get out for a while, but in most cases to no avail. Alan Derek finally manages to put an act of desperation as if he's desperate for the toilet, holding his crotch and clenching his teeth, this is only because he's observed other kids doing it for real. It works as Margaret says to him.

"you have two minutes and you better get straight back".

Of course, he has no intension of going to the toilet. As he walks towards the door, he glances over to Archie; he clearly gets the message and copies Alan Derek's actions.

"you can wait till he returns" she tells him,

"but miss" Archie says as the door closes.

Alan Derek makes his way to the hallway which connects to the stairwell and another narrower hallway that lead to the main entrance. As he reaches the stairwell he's met by Joyce,

"can you help me carry some things upstairs".

she says struggling to carry a heap of clothes,

"yes" he replies,

she places the clothes on the table in the hallway, separating a small bundle enough for Alan Derek to carry.

"You carry this".

she says as she puts the small bundle on his stretched-out arms. She then picks up the remaining bundle.

"We're just going to take them upstairs then you can go back to the playroom, ok".

"yes" Alan Derek replies with reluctance.

As they get to the foot of the stairs, Margaret emerges from the playroom and with a furious tone to her voice says,

"WHAT ON EARTH DO YOU THINK YOU ARE DOING HERE",

Joyce intervenes politely saying,

"I asked him to help me".

At that point she grabs Alan Derek's left arm pulling him back causing the clothes in his arms to fall to the floor. Joyce lets the clothes she's carrying drop as she grabs his right arm.

"I TOLD YOU HE'S HELPING ME, NOW LET GO" she says, as she pulls.

"NO, YOU LET GO"

Margaret replies still pulling on his left arm. Alan Derek is in the midst of being dragged back and forth mostly in the direction of the play hall. Although he finds it uncomfortable, he finds it amusing being used as a tool of tug of war in a battle of supremacy between two staff members. With all the excitement and noise, it attracts the attention of the others in the Playroom as they pop their heads out the door to see what is going on. Archie and the others are laughing at the live entertainment taking place in front of them catching the attention of Margaret. With that, she let's go.

"Make sure he comes back to the room when you're done".

she tells Joyce in a more subdued manner. Joyce nods yes, Margaret turns towards the Play hall door.

"GET BACK ON THOSE BENCHES" she shouts to the others,

followed by their heads shooting back into the room. Alan Derek looks at Joyce, she looks back at him.

"Are you ok" she says as she smiles,

Alan Derek already smiling knowing the battle is won replies,

"yes"

"I'm sorry you had to go through that". Joyce says,

With that they both pick up the fallen clothes and head upstairs. Shortly after, they both return to the Playroom. As they enter, Margaret tells him to get back to the corner. As he walks to the end, he keeps looking back as Margaret gives him an evil look. After sitting down, he looks over to his friend Archie, they smile at each other only this time he doesn't care if they are being watched.

Chapter 5
The Wicked Witch

The days and nights are colder, and Halloween has come. It's Alan Derek's first Halloween party and the older kids are also having their party, so the younger ones have to go down to the porta cabin for theirs as the older kids need more space. The party is held in the staff room at the Porta cabin as that room is smaller and warmer, and with just half a dozen younger kids, it's enough space. It's fun with apple dunk etc, until one staff member thought it would be funny putting a witch's mask on and popping her head from outside the back window which looks in from a small wooded area. Not the ideal thing to do to a bunch of two to four-year olds, as they all freak out screaming mercilessly prompting the staff to panic trying to calm them down resulting in the party finishing early.

"Ok" Joyce said,

pausing for a moment, then adding,

"get into pairs",

With that, everyone complies still shaking by the incident moments ago with some still sniffling from the crying. They head to the door. Just as Joyce opens it Margaret walks in as they're about to leave for the winding walk back up to the main house. No one moves,

"come on".

Margaret says nudging one of the kids towards the door. They're in tears again as no-one wants to move. They're terrified of the witch coming back. Margaret is getting impatient,

"GET A MOVE ON" she said angrily,

but still, no one is moving. She grabs the hand of the boy in front trying to pull him, but his hand slips from her grasp and he runs into the play area. The rest follows.

"They're terrified, you shouldn't have done that",

Joyce tells Margaret, a clear indication she had something to do with scaring them.

"It was only a bit of fun" Margaret replies,

"they don't seem to think it was" she responds.

"Well, we have to get them up to the house" Margaret says.

"Lindsey, come with me".

Joyce says to another much younger staff member. They both go outside and after a minute Joyce walks back in without Lindsey.

"Where's she gone" Margaret asks,

"I've sent her to get help" she replies.

Margret is speaking softly with Joyce. There's a bit of an argument going on and Margaret is clearly not happy with Joyce taking control. Ten minutes later, a dozen of the older kids walk in lead by Lindsey. Each takes a hand of the younger kids. Joyce takes one of Alan Derek's hand, whilst one of the older girls take his other.

"Right, we're going up to the main house, ok".

Joyce says as the boys in the front open the door with each of the younger kids between two older kids. The older kids are not that much older than the younger kids, with only a couple of years between them, but it's enough to give them the confidence to walk to the main building, though the younger kids are still traumatised by the earlier experience. They constantly look around fearful the witch might still be out there totally unaware the witch is right behind them in the form of Margaret. Finally reaching the main house, the youngsters are taken straight up to bed with some waking up crying throughout the night, and being cared for by Joyce and other staff members with Margaret nowhere to be seen.

Chapter 6
The First Move

It's a month after the new year. It's February 1969, and Alan Derek has just turned four. It is a cold early winters morning when he leaves the doors of Blairvadach for the last time. The condensation which leaves his mouth as he walks to the waiting taxi, forms clouds like the smoke that exhales from the mouths of some of the staff who smoked throughout his stay. He gets into the waiting taxi with his escort, one he does not know nor has he seen at the home before. The taxi sets off down the winding road that he has walked on many times passing the porta cabin for the last time down to the gate. As he approaches the gate, he looks back at the partially exposed house covered by trees and bushes which now looks like a castle from the angle he's at as he passes through the gates he thought he would never leave. It's all new to him. He's never been in a car before and at four years old he's excited by his surroundings. He takes a last glance at the building site he spent most of last summer observing from the front lawn, never to see its completion. He looks at the driver occasionally turning a large wheel in front of him, feeling the bumps with every pothole the wheels hit along the route. He pulls his small frame up clutching the base of the window, looking out to see the beautiful parts of Scotland he is about to leave. Even though he's still young and only beginning to learn about his surroundings, he's overwhelmed by the natural beauty that lay beyond the glass protecting him from the elements as the car drives along the road. This was to be a factor in years to come for his love for the outdoors, and his sanctuary to forget his past from what was to come as he progressed through his childhood years.

As he looks to his right over the wide opening of the river Clyde, he's confronted by the distant mist from the morning sun partially covering the ships and trawlers that are either returning or setting off for their morning runs. As he looks to his left, the natural beauty of Scotland catches his eyes as the hilltops that were until now partially blocked by trees during his time in the home, are now finally in full view glossed in a beautiful layer of frost sparkling as the sun bounces off the crystals that form them with some jade grass poking through. The sky is blue with few clouds to see. And the stoned houses that look stunning dotted along the hillside.

As the Taxi drives along the road, the river is narrowing, and the hills are becoming smaller. The ships are getting bigger as they come closer, with small boats, rowers, and dinghies dotted along the banks of the river Clyde. He kneels on the back seat looking out the back window watching as the world he leaves disappears into the distance. The trip feels long, but in reality it's only an hour or so. As the taxi stops for the lights, he hears a familiar sound. It's getting louder and passes his eyes at speed. Carriage after carriage, as he gets excited at the fact he's finally solved the mystery of the invisible sound he's constantly heard coming from behind the trees that blocked his view from the back of the Home as far back as he remembers, seeing for the first time a train heading towards the home he just left travelling across the hills.

They carry on going from open spaced-out houses, to more tightly rows of buildings as they approach Glasgow. Factories, tenements, and shops fill the spaces, with the smell of coal fires filling the air as chimney after chimney spew the ruminants that keep their dwellers warm. The taxi turns off the busy roads where a mixture of red and green busses, lorries, and cars run in both directions. The roads they turn into becomes quieter, with fewer cars and less noise from the Diesel engines other than that of the taxi as it drives further. Soon they reach their destination. The taxi stops and as he looks out, he sees that all the houses are red and neatly lined up on both sides of the street unlike the houses he saw earlier, or that of where he had come from, which were all made with uneven stone. None of which had straight lines like the brickwork he now sees.

The house he's about to move into is a small semi-detached house with a small garden that leads to the front door. As they enter it has narrow stairs to the left and two doors to the right, one leading to the lounge and the other leading to the kitchen. And one straight ahead leading to the Bathroom. He meets the couple for the first time, Jack and Brenda with their two dogs. They are a good couple and this is to be his new home, or so he hopes. They have no children, but own two dogs, one small the other big, but not too big. The dogs are fine at first until later that night when Alan Derek is being changed for bed in the living room by Brenda in front of the warm crackling coal fire. The bigger dog starts barking, then without any warning attacks Alan Derek followed by the other smaller dog. Brenda manages to keep Alan Derek away from their growling jaws. Seeing someone else in the house and being pampered triggers a jealous feeling with the dogs as they are clearly taking a dislike to him having all the attention in that moment. pouncing on him at every opportunity. growling, causing Alan Derek to panic with fear of being bitten. Things get so bad the dogs are taken into the kitchen and are not allowed in the same room as Alan Derek. Jack, trying to ease his young fearful mind tells him.

"they'll get use to you in time".

with the situation calm now, Brenda finishes changing him. It's bedtime now and Brenda leads the way. Up they go, up the uncarpeted stairs as the noise of crackling boards from the bare wooden stairs beat out under their feet. The dogs are no fool as they bark knowing their unwelcome intruder is still hogging most of the house they would often wonder freely through. They enter the bedroom which is the first door at the top of the stairs. It's tiny compared to what Alan Derek is used to with just a single low-level bed against the right wall and barely any room for anything else.

"I've never had a room to myself".

Alan Derek remarks as he walks the short distance to the bed.

"well, you have it all to yourself now"

replies Brenda as she opens the covers of the bed for Alan Derek to slip into. Brenda tucks him in as he shivers in the cold bed with no central heating in the room.

"I'll put the heater on".

Brenda says as she stretches over the bed reaching for the pull cord attached to an electric heater high above the wall. As she puts it on it glows bright orange letting little heat fill the room.

"you'll soon warm up"

she says as Jack enters the room with a hot water bottle placing it by his small cold feet under his blankets, giving him some extra comfort.

"I'll come back later to switch the heater off"

Jack says, with both leaving the room saying goodnight, leaving the door slightly ajar, and with no babies crying, he manages to get a peaceful night's sleep.

"Wake up" a voice says softly,

"wake up Alan".

a bit louder as Alan Derek comes out of his sleep,

"it's time to get up" Brenda says as she opens the curtains.

"Put your slippers on and come downstairs, breakfast is ready",

she says as she leaves the room,

"can I go to the toilet".

he says as he hurriedly puts his slippers on desperately needing to wee.

"Of course, you can"

replies Brenda as she carries on walking downstairs with Alan Derek quickly running behind, held up by her slow walk down the narrow stairs, realising these narrow stairs unlike the wide stairs at the home are a problem. As soon as they hit the bottom, he rushes into the toilet the moment he sees a gap between her and the bottom of the step. Out he comes heading to the lounge and being grabbed by Jack just as he gets to the door.

"Breakfast is in the kitchen; the dogs are in there" referring to the lounge.

Just as he walks into the kitchen a small table is butted up against the wall with three chairs on the remaining sides. To the side is a small cooker, sink and a few free-standing cabinets.

"Alan, what would you like for breakfast".

Brenda asks no longer adding the second part of his name,

"Cornflakes please" he replies,

"you don't mind me calling you just Alan do you, it's much easier" she adds,

"no"

he replies whilst shrugging his shoulders and receiving his bowl of cornflakes.

"Would you like tea with that" Brenda added,

"don't you have lunch before tea" he replies,

both Jack and Brenda laugh. Alan looks at them with confusion trying to figure out what it was he said they found funny. After a while when they stopped, Brenda explains the tea was referring to the hot drink, something Alan had never had or heard of until now.

"Would you like to try some" Brenda asks,

after pausing and looking at the steam coming from the cup she's drinking from, Alan replies,

"yes please".

Brenda pours him half a cup as he sits watching the hot almost black liquid pour from the spout of the kettle amazed at the sight of the steam rising as the liquid falls mid air. She pours milk in and adds a teaspoon full of sugar. Alan stares at the cup before picking it up and putting it to his lips. Slowly he tips the cup feeling the heat as the hot liquid get closer to his lips.

"Be careful it's hot" Brenda says,

He takes a sip then put the cup down as his face skews from the disgusting taste.

"Can I have a glass of milk please".

Alan asks as he pushes the cup still full of tea away from him.

Just as breakfast finishes, Brenda still washing up says.

"Jack, can you show Alan his toothbrush".

Jack was busy reading his newspaper before raising his head towards Brenda.

"ok dear"

He says as he folds back the page he was reading and placing the newspaper on the now cleared table.

"Follow me"

he says getting up from the table and walking to the door. Alan follows and both go into the bathroom. On the narrow shelf above the sink is a brand new toothbrush still in its packaging, Jack takes it and removes the packing revealing a small toothbrush, he rinses it under the open tap, then squeezes a small amount of toothpaste onto its bristles.

"off you go, start brushing",

He says as he leaves closing the door behind him. Within a matter of seconds he hears the dogs on the other side of the door, one starts growling, then barks, with Jack's voice telling it to be quiet. Then he hears the sound of the kitchen door closing as Jack takes them in from the lounge.

It doesn't take long for Alan to finish brushing his teeth, partly because he's never done it before. He opens the bathroom door; jack sees his mouth is covered in toothpaste.

"you need to rinse your mouth".

jack says as he escorts him back into the bathroom. After rinsing his mouth, he makes his way into the lounge where Brenda is waiting with his clothes laid out neatly ready to change him from his pyjamas. For most of the day they sit in the lounge listening to radio programs as TVs are a luxury they could not afford. Alan has never seen a TV nor heard a radio even whilst living in the Home, so its no loss to him. Just the boredom of not having his friends there to play with, something that did not take him a day to realise. He understood nothing that was being said or played on the radio and spent most of the morning twiddling his fingers. At least that is how it felt to him, as there were no toys or other kids around to play with. Lunch is served in the lounge rather than moving the dogs around. After lunch Jack takes the dogs out for a walk, something Alan longed to do just to kill the boredom despite the freezing cold weather and would have if not for the dogs wanting to eat him at every opportunity.

Soon Jack returns and puts the dogs back into the kitchen. Brenda tells Alan to put his shoes and coat on.

"ah good, going out, just hope he doesn't put that thing round my neck" he thinks to himself as he looks at the dogs leashes still in the grasp of Jacks hand, and then with a sigh of relief as he places them on the sideboard.

"Are you ready" says Jack,

"yes" he replies.

Then off they go, out the gate and up the road to the bus

stop on to a waiting bus.

"Jump on" Jack says in an excited voice,

they go in from the back of the bus as the conductor stands with his hand on a cord waiting for them all to get on, before pulling it sounding a bell to instruct the driver to go. By then his bell phobia was a distant memory.

"Have you ever been on a bus before".

Jack asks, trying to build up a conversation,

"no" Alan replies,

"we travel by bus a lot, but occasionally use a taxi, but they're not cheap",

says Jack. It's clear Jack's trying to build up a relationship with Alan though he's too young to understand that. Brenda watches on as Jack continues to talk, occasionally smiling as he tries to joke. Soon the conversation is interrupted by the bell as Brenda gets to her feet with Jack and Alan following.

They get off the bus. Alan is overwhelmed with the crowd, and the shops that line the street, with the huge buses tailgating one another. This was something he'd never seen before after spending four years in a compound away from any city, with only a few vehicles passing on the main road periodically. The first shop they enter is to get new clothes. Alan is measured up by the keeper and tries various clothes on, then leaving with Jack carrying a couple of bags. Still on the same side of the road, they walk past a sweet shop, Alan's eyes pop wide open seeing the sugary delights openly enticing his sweet tooth to signal his brain into an early teenagers' defiant tendency pulling his hand from Brenda to raid this sweet bank. Brenda clearly gets the message, and without hesitation she takes the lead, and into the shop they go. With so much to choose from, a bag of mixed sweets are bought and handed to Alan to munch as they walk. More shops are visited, though more to do with food, and of course, every child's heaven, the toy shop,

"is there anything you like".

Brenda asks with a huge smile on her face as they walk around. There are huge toys all over. Rocking horses, metal trucks, cars, small toy soldiers, but the one thing that catches Alan's eye is a small torch in the clutches of another boy's hand testing the light beam as he shines it around the shop.

"Can I have that please".

Alan asks politely to Brenda,

"aye" she replies,

She picks up the item from a box on the counter with some batteries to go with it. She asks Jack to take him to the cafe a couple of doors away whilst she pays for the torch. A few minutes later, she turns up to the cafe with more bags. When she sits down, she hands the torch to Jack asking him to put the batteries in, then he passes it to Alan showing him how it works.

As they have tea, the light is starting to fade outside. Alan is getting excited at the prospect of using his new torch, and as they leave the café, he's disappointed by the brightness on the street from the bright lights coming from the shops. They get on to the bus making their way back, and as they get off the bus to walk back down the street to the house, Alan's face immediately lights up as he can now use his new torch on the dimly lit street. He takes the lead walking a few paces in front of the couple, swinging the torch, creating a beam of light like a disco ball, and as he does, he notices snowflakes falling in front of the light beam.

"Jack look" he says with excitement,

"what is it" Says Jack,

"it's snow" he says as Jack gets closer to Alan,

"Brenda, he's right, it is snowing" says Jack.

They get home. Jack and Alan go into the lounge whilst Brenda empties most of the bags in the kitchen. After a few minutes, she walks into the lounge with two more bags placing them in front of the fire that is still warming up after Jack lit it, and starts emptying the contents of the bag in front of Alan. It wasn't just the clothes she bought him earlier whilst they were in the cafe. She went on a spending spree buying him plenty of toys, more than enough to take away any boredom like what he felt earlier in the day, or at least that may have been the intention. Day three, and lying on the floor belly down, Alan is playing with his new cars. By mid day he's feeling lost, missing his friends, especially Archie and is now struggling to adapt to his new surroundings. The house is an average family home, but not as big and spacious like what he was used to. With no one to play with, and pretty much confined to the lounge in fear of the dogs. Both Jack and Brenda are picking up on his sadness as he would constantly gaze at the window, then stop and stare at the toys but not play with them.

Alan can hear them whispering to each other but can't make out what they are saying. Moments later, Jack gets up and heads towards the door as Brenda tells Alan to come and sit next to her on the settee. As soon as he does, she looks at him and says,

"whatever happens, don't be scared, remain calm and don't say anything".

at that moment, the dogs come into the lounge. With no hesitations they go straight over to where Alan is sitting. He pushes himself into Brenda's side. His heart is racing as the dogs' bark and growl. Even though both Brenda and Jack are telling the dogs to shut up and sit, they are not heeding the instructions. The bigger dog lunges at Alan, grabbing his foot with his mouth and taking his slightly oversized slipper clean off. A little higher and it would have been his foot. Jack grabs the bigger dog by the collar dragging him out of the room whilst ordering the smaller dog to follow. As soon as they're out of the room, Brenda raps her arms around Alan trying to comfort him as he continues to shake uncontrollable, and crying.

That same night Alan struggles to sleep. He's having nightmares of being eaten by the dogs. Both Brenda and Jack take it in turns to calm him down, but two days later a social worker turns up. The Couple had made the decision to remove Alan from the situation. It's clear the dogs are not taking to Alan. They are left with a choice, and sadly for Alan, they chose the dogs over him, and it was only a matter of time before he would have to move on. So, in less than a week Alan is smartly dressed up in light blue dungaree style shorts which he absolutely hates. A new shirt and jumper, and brand-new sandals. Brenda sits him down and explains to him saying,

"Both I and Jack desperately wanted things to work out. You were always polite when we took you to the shops. You asked for nothing apart from one thing. If things were different, we would love to have kept you",

At that point Alan still only four, knew what was coming.

"the dogs are not accepting you, and we are more fearful of you getting hurt. Because of that, Christine will be taking you to another home".

The only reply Alan gives is,

"ok"

partly because he's too young to understand everything. He is glad he's getting away from the dogs, but deep down he's disappointed that he came second. He did like the couple, but he knew he had no control over the situation. They walk Alan to the door. Christine and Jack take his things.

Brenda picks up a few bags placing them in front of Alan. It's the toys they bought for him a few days ago. Brenda looks at him then says,

"we bought these toys for you; I want you to keep them".

"Thank you" he replies.

Then they make their way to the waiting taxi.

Chapter 7
Eversley Children's Home

So, in less than a week, Alan is back in a taxi waving as he leaves, only this time no countryside to pass, just buildings dotted and bunched together along the route with some open space and more smoked filled skies from the chimneys along his route even though he's not taking as much notice of the journey as he did last week, upset over the situation he's found himself in.

It is a much shorter journey than a week ago as they turn onto Aytoun Road. The houses along both sides are big and detached and run along the road with a row of trees along the pavement. They finally reach their destination. The home named Eversley Children's Home, is situated in an up-market part of Glasgow set on Aytoun Rd Pollokshields. It's one of the largest houses on the street classified as a mansion. It has two driveway gates, one to drive through, and the other to exit. The driveway curves from one to the other. The house is large though not as large as his previous Home. It has a large front garden.

The house is cream in colour on the outside front, with two full size symmetrical bay windows on either side of the main entrance door, covering both floors. There are extended buildings on either side of the main building, the one on the left built sometime later after its original build. The entrance door is a large green single door which leads to a small foyer and to a second larger panelled windowed door. As they walk through both doors, they enter a large hallway with a long sideboard situated to the right before the door that leads to the nursery. The door to the left leads to the dining room. Towards the back of the entrance hall are the stairs which are double the width of a normal staircase, but similar in width to Blairvadach, with a platform set below a large window overseeing the large rear garden and a right 180 turn to get to the first floor, which has two large bedrooms at the front sleeping seven in each. A slightly smaller which sleeps five, and a further two which sleeps three in each. The office is situated between the two largest bedrooms at the front of the house.

Alan is shown to his room, the one that sleeps five. The social worker who accompanied him on the trip and the Matron help carry his luggage up and lay them on his bed,

"wait here, someone will come and help you unpack".

Matron tells him before leaving with the social worker. Alan sits on the high bed, similar to the bed he had at Blairvadach children's home. Next to him is a large single wardrobe. He walks over to the window overlooking the huge back garden that goes all the way back to the main road Albert Drive, shielded by an eight-foot-high brick wall with a closed green gate dead centre. A rough, uneven path goes around close to the perimeter dividing the main grass area from a narrower border strip leading to the perimeter wall. A sand pit at the bottom right-side corner, and swings directly in front of him. Unlike his previous home where the huge front garden was sloping down from the building, this garden is mostly flat with two small hills. One from the hard ground below the window, and the other from the right side of the garden close to the mobile unit that holds children waiting for spaces either at Eversley or other homes across Scotland. The one thing missing from the garden are the kids. He hears the door opening as it creaks from the un-lubricated hinges turning around to the sight of a large woman with dark curly hair walking in.

"you must be Alan" she says,

"yes" he replies,

"hello, my name is Moreen, now let's get you unpacked",

she says as she walks over to his bed.

She opens his suitcase laying everything neatly on the bed, then picks up the bags full of toys.

"that a lot of toys"

she says as she takes them out one by one,

"Brenda gave them to me" he replies,

"she must have been kind" Moreen responded,

with Alan responding with a nod.

"I'll put these in the bottom of the wardrobe",

Moreen says, as she begins putting them in the wardrobe next to his bed. With his clothes still on the bed, she turns to him and says,

"you might as well change in to some other clothes",

taking a pair of jeans a t-shirt and a jumper from the unpacked suitcase and putting them to the side. Alan quickly changes into the laid-out clothes glad to get out of those dungaree shorts he hated so much. Moreen puts the rest of his clothes in the wardrobe,

"it's almost lunch time" Moreen says,

"I'll take you to the dining room then show you around after lunch" she continues to say.

As they walk towards the door, Moreen notices him holding his trouser up,

"do you need a belt" she asks,

"what's that" he replies,

"to hold your trousers up"

pointing to his waist as he struggles to hold them,

"Aye" he responds,

they leave the room, walk downstairs, then turn to the back of the stairs where a row of cupboard doors are situated along the back wall. Moreen opens the door and pulls a red and white snake belt out putting it around his waist through the loops on his trousers waistband, then adjusting the side buckle.

"Is that better" she asks him,

"yes" he replies.

"Come on then, follow me, I'll take you to the dining room"

she says as she passes him walking the few metres to the room where tables are laid out with cutlery. Other children are walking in through the door directly opposite the door they just walked in. Some in school uniform, and some just in plain clothes. There's a hatch on the wall between both doors on the right separating the Dining room from a small kitchen mainly used to keep the food warm. The dining room isn't full as some go to the infant's school which is a distance away. Some of the younger non school age children are about the same age as Alan, with some primary school age children from Pollokshields Primary school, which is just around the corner from the home who walk the short distance for lunch. They sit at the tables looking at Alan whilst whispering to each other and eating,

"sit here",

Moreen says pointing to an empty chair by a table with three other children roughly his age,

"are you new here",

says a voice opposite him on the same table, he looks over, it's a young girl,

"yes" he replies,

she continues,

"what's your name".

"Alan" he replies,

"my name's Rosemary, but everyone calls me Rose".

she says with a smile on her face. The boy sitting to his right, a little shorter asks,

"why is your hair so black".

Alan glancing his eyes upwards as if he could see his hair replies with the words,

"I don't know",

the interrogation continues,

"are you coming in the playroom" Rose asks,

"I don't know" Alan replies,

"where did you come from" the boy next to him asks,

Alan shrugs his shoulders as if to say, "I don't know".

The interrogation continues until lunch is over after which, the kids get up and go through the door they came through for lunch. Alan sits waiting for Moreen to return. The Dining room is now empty with just the cooks clearing up and wiping the tables down. Moments later Moreen walks through.

"did you enjoy your lunch" she asks,

"yes" he replies,

"good, follow me, I'll show you around",

she says as she heads towards the other door. Alan follows. Moreen opens the door holding it open for Alan to walk through. She points to the door on the right.

"that door leads to the back garden".

she says, opening it but not going out. There's a few steps just outside the door leading into the garden. She closes the door, then looking straight ahead there are a few steps to climb.

"mind the steps" she says,

At the top she points to the doorless room to the right,

"that's the cloakroom".

She says walking up a few more steps to get in.

"I'll bring your coat down later and show you where to put it" she tells him.

Coming out they walk a few feet further. Moreen points to the door on the right,

"that's the girls toilets".

she says, then takes him left just after the girls toilets to a smaller corridor that leads to the other front door and the boys toilet.

"that's the door you'll be using most of the time and not the main door, and this door to the right is the boys toilets" she says, they turn back towards the girls toilets and directly opposite the girls toilet door leads to the play room. Moreen opens the door. There are a dozen kids all about the same age. The playroom is about the same size, almost identical to the the Play hall at Blairvadach, with a row of built in benches around the entire room, with the exception of the far end wall. on one side of the wall, there are windows running the full length of the wall. The wall to the right, has no windows, but still has built in benches running that entire wall. At the back two windows on either side of an emergency door that leads to a small foyer with another door leading to the rear garden via stairs.

"ALAN"

a familiar voice shouts out. Alan looks over to its origins. It's Rose with a big smile on her face as she runs over to him. Alan looks away too shy to acknowledge her.

"it's me, Rosemary".

Alan glances at her again then looks at Moreen hoping to be rescued. Too late, Rose is in front of him,

"do you want to play" she says,

Alan still shy doesn't respond. But then the boy who was interrogating him at the table at lunch walks over to him, he also just happens to have the same name Alan, though his last name is McKenzie.

"Play with us",

he says as he dances back over to his friends,

"ok" he replies, following him.

"Hello" Jimmy says,

"Hello" Alan replies,

"wots your name" Jimmy asks,

"Alan" he replies,

"that's his name" pointing to Alan McKenzie,

"I know" he replies,

with a smile,

"let's play tig",

Frank says, the other boy with them.

"Ok" all set,

"you're on",

Alan Mckenzie tells Alan,

"what do I do" he asks,

"have you no played the game before" Alan McKenzie asks,

"no" he replies,

"you have to count to ten, then chase us, if you tig someone they're on".

"ok"

pausing for a bit then adding after thinking

"how do I tig" Alan says,

"you just touch one of us" Frank says,

"OK",

"count" Jimmy says,

"ok" they all start running,

"one, two, four"

He carries on counting completely out of sequence, until his name is called.

"Alan come here",

Moreen shouts to grab his attention over the noise. Both Alans approach,

"no, not you"

she says to Alan McKenzie. Barbara the other staff member says to Moreen,

"this could be a problem",

"yes, and they're both in the same bedroom" she replies,

as they giggle,

"Alan, this is Barbara, she'll be looking after you in here, ok"

"yes" he replies,

"you can carry on playing" she says before leaving the room.

"Start counting again" Alan McKenzie says as he returns to them.

"MCKENZIE, GET OVER HERE RIGHT NOW" Barbara shouts,

Alan startled by her shout looks around seeing Alan McKenzie walking over pleading,

"it was an accident miss; I didn't mean to do it"

Rosemary's friend is in tears,

"YOU RAN RIGHT INTO HER" Barbara rants on

"GET OVER HERE"

Alan McKenzie is already beginning to cry as he continues to walk over,

"it was an accident" he repeated,

Barbara looks around shouting,

"THE REST OF YOU SIT ON THE BENCH"

pointing over to the benches lined up along the windows. Alan is already having memories of Margaret from his previous home, seeing some similarities, but as he sits down, she carries on shouting at Alan McKenzie,

"FACE THAT WALL AND TAKE YOUR TROUSERS DOWN"

Still protesting he didn't mean to do it,

"DON'T MAKE ME COME OVER THERE" she shouts,

reluctantly he follows her instructions with his back to the rest of the kids as he faces the wall dropping his trousers slowly, Alan is shaken by this.

"what could he have done that was so bad",

thinking to himself as he observed. His thoughts are that Margaret never went to these extremes of telling the kids to drop their trousers.

"NOW STAND THERE AND DON'T SAY A WORD".

then turning to the rest

"that goes for you too" in a slightly calmer tone.

It feels forever but after about 5 minutes she orders him to pull his trousers up, then still teary eyed he joins the rest of his friends.

"Why did she do that" Alan asks,

"she usually spanks us when she tells us to pull our trousers down" Frank says.

For most of that afternoon everyone remains subdued, with Alan still not understanding what that was all about.

Chapter 8
New Friends

The older kids are back from school and changed into their normal clothes before joining Alan and the other kids in the Playroom. The younger ones go to the side where they mostly sit including Alan to keep out of the older boys way. A few of them are staring at him. They walk over, one of them not much taller than Alan stands in front of him.

"what's your name" he says with a little smirk on his face,

"Alan" he replies,

"that's his name" pointing to Alan McKenzie who is sitting next to him,

"I Know" Alan replies,

"what's your name" Alan asks, responding to him,

"Peter" he replies, there's a slight pause,

"Do you want to hear a story" Peter asks,

Alan looks at Alan McKenzie, he has a smile on his face, and nods to Alan to say yes. He looks back to Peter,

"aye" he replies,

"ok let me sit there".

Both Alan and Alan McKenzie move slightly in opposite direction to each other to let Peter slip in. The others gather around all with big cheesy smiles on their faces. Alan begins to smile even though he has no idea why.

"Right" Peter says just as he's about to go into his story.

"Gilamashina"

he starts with and then narrates a story with Gilamashina as his character. He has everyone in laughter as he continues for a good ten minutes. After he finishes Alan asks,

"who's Gilamashina",

"no one" Peter responds,

"he's just a made-up name" he adds,

"that was funny" Alan said,

Peter pauses, looks at Alan and the other kids with him,

"do you want to play" he asks,

"yes"

a joint response from them. And off they go playing together till tea time..

The call has come for tea and everyone walks the short distance to the dining room. Alan sits at the same table he sat at during lunch,

"ALAN"

a voice shouts from behind,

"PETER, keep your voice down, there's no need to shout",

says another voice from near the hatch. Alan looks back. Peter grabs his attention as he waves his hand softly saying,

"come over here",

Alan looks at his friends. Alan McKenzie says

"don't go, stay here".

Alan looks back, Peter is still waving his hand calling him over, Alan turns back,

"I like him, he's funny",

he says to his new friends. He looks around the table and all of them are staring at him with long faces while still seeing Peter trying to call him,

"go" Alan McKenzie tells him.

He stands up and walks over to Peter's table joining him for tea. After a while Moreen walked in,

"right, you lot, let's get you ready for bed"

directing her comments to the first two tables where Alan McKenzie sits. They get up starting to make there way to the door, "where's Alan" she asks,

Alan McKenzie points over to the table in the middle of the room,

"over there with Peter" he tells her,

Moreen looks over. Alan is already looking at her which he's done since she walked in just hoping she'll let him stay a little longer.

"come on" she tells him,

he gets up making his way to the door joining the others.

"see you later",

Peter says as Alan walks through the door held open by Moreen as she stands waiting for him. Alan looks back, smiles and walks off without comment. Walking from the dining room to the stairs Moreen looks at Alan saying,

"I see you've made friends" referring to Peter,

"aye" he replied,

Moreen giving him a stern look,

"hmmm"

Alan immediately realising she did not like his reply, correcting it by saying,

"yes"

"that's better" she replies.

"Has he told you the story about Gilamashina yet",

Alan laughs,

"Aye, I mean yes" he replies,

continuing to say

"he's funny".

Moreen looking at him saying,

"yes, I know".

she isn't concerned with him being friends with Peter who's older, probably because they're both similar in height with Alan being tall for his age. Alan's room is at the top of the stairs. The first room to his right. As he walks over, the bathroom door which is next to his room is open and two children younger than him are in the bath with bubbles playing as two staff members are bathing them. It's unmissable as it's directly next to his bedroom door. He walks into his room behind Moreen, and to his excitement sees his new friends in the same room. Alan McKenzie, Frank, Jimmy and another boy he hadn't met till now, John, a schoolboy in his first year. And so ends his first day at his new home fitting in quite well with his new friends in an environment he's already use to from his time at Blairvadach. Archie now becoming just a distant memory.

Early rise is the norm in Children's home. Even non-

School starters have to be up at the same time as the schoolers.

"Come on boys, wake up".

barely awake, Alan's eyes open to the sight of Moreen opening the curtains.

"come on, up you get",

her voice again forcing them out of their semi-conscious state. John is already up and changing into his School Uniform as the rest of them are still too laid back to get up, though Moreen is having none of it and walks round to each bed pulling the bed sheets down to their feet.

"Come on",

she says in a long slow jokingly tone, adding,

"you won't get any breakfast".

enough for them to shoot out of bed and change into their clothes.

"Frank, your T-shirt is inside out".

she says as she walks over to him and helps him put it right whilst the others laugh. John has already left the room on his way to the dining room as Moreen get the rest of them ready then marches them down. Halfway down they meeting up with Rose and the other girls on the stairs. Rose is a few steps in front looking back, "hello Alan" she says,

Alan acknowledging with a nod whilst the others start teasing him.

"she likes you" Jimmy says,

Alan looks at Jimmy with an expression of yuck on his face. All three boys laugh. They enter the dining room. Alan is looking around for Peter but he's nowhere to be seen as he's already left for school. After breakfast they're back in the playroom which is pretty much their daily routine. The next week or two goes pretty much as the first day, though Barbara still humiliates everyone in the playroom, both boys and girls.

It's late March, the nights are getting longer. The sun is warmer and for the first time, Alan goes into the back garden. It's huge. He watches as the top of the double decker busses pass the high wall at the bottom of the garden which leads on to the main road though the gate is never opened. The grass is still damp from the cold spring nights. He runs to the swings and sits on it facing the house. He's taken in by the huge window that covers the staircase as it stands out amongst the others completely offset from the symmetry of the building and other windows. To his left a mobile unit situated outside the kitchen door. Beyond that, a separate building that houses the Matron with her disabled daughter who suffers from multiple sclerosis, though in her late teens she gets on great with the kids. Part of the same outer building is also used as a youth club for the school aged kids. To his right the Playroom where he spent most of his days till this point. Moreen is on the hard surface talking to Barbara, they're smiling, she periodically looks over to Alan, he's wondering if he's in trouble. Moreen is pointing over to him whilst talking, but the distance is that far he can't hear them. Moreen walk over to his direction. Alan is becoming nervous, unsure what he's done wrong,

"are you not swinging" she asks,

Alan unable to hear her properly replies,

"wot"

"are you not swinging, and it's pardon not wot", she replies,

"I don't know how to" he says,

she's reaches him,

"have you not been on a swing before" she asks,

"no" he replies,

"shall I push you" she asks,

"yes please"

she starts pushing him. His stomach feels weird as he goes up both ways. He's midair on only a seat held up by two chains. He fears for a moment that he'll fall off it, as he remembers the scooter incident,

"STOP" he shouts,

"it's ok, you're perfectly safe" she says,

"NO PLEASE STOP"

he replies as he gets agitated. She slows it down but doesn't stop,

"is this ok" she asks,

"yes" he replied.

She lets the swing go still swinging slightly and sits on the swing next to him even though it's clearly tight for her large size,

"Alan, are you ok" she asks,

"yes" he replies,

"why were you scared" she asks,

"I thought I was going to fall" he replies,

"it wasn't high" she said,

"I know".

then explaining about his last fall off the scooter. She laughed. Not at his memory, but that she understood his fear.

"there's no need to get scared",

she says as she gets off the swing with a little bit of effort, then adding, "we'll try again, and you say when to stop and I won't push any higher, ok"

"ok" he replies nervously,

by now he's getting more confident. Moreen continues talking to him keeping his mind off the swinging and asking about his previous home. He's seeing a likeness from Moreen to that of Joyce the staff member from his previous home. He likes Moreen, and it's clear she likes him.

It's Easter. With Alan and his friends being so young, not much is made of the day as they're still too young to understand its meaning. They're only given a chocolate Easter egg to signify it whilst they watch as the older kids roll decorated chicken eggs down the small hilly verge outside the back garden. The kids are laughing and celebrating as they teas their friends whose eggs break, just having fun. When the egg role is over, Alan and his friends are escorted back into the playroom with sticky hands and covered mouths from the melting chocolate.

Summer has arrived its May. It's only weeks away till the other kids break up from school for the Summer holidays, except on this day it's anything but Summer. It's dull, wet and windy. Alan and the other kids are stuck indoors. Barbara is having a bad day. She's shouting at everyone. No one is immune, including Alan. Everyone is making the best of the day, playing tig, all including the girls,

"KEEP YOUR NOISE DOWN" Barbara shouts,

Alan laughs loudly after seeing Frank trip almost falling to the ground,

"GET OVER HERE ALAN NAVSA" she shouts,

"YOU TOO FRANK"

who laughed in response to Alan's laughter just at the moment Barbara shouted, both making their way over,

"THE REST OF YOU SIT ON THE BENCHES"

a procedure everyone has gotten so use too.

"WHEN I TELL YOU TO BE QUIET, YOU DO EXACTLY THAT. NOW FACE THE WALL AND DROP YOUR TROUSERS, BOTH OF YOU"

both Alan and Frank stand next to each other. They look at each other then look around to the rest of the kids feeling embarrassed at that request,

"I WON'T TELL YOU AGAIN"

both drop their trousers, still facing the wall whilst blushing knowing there's a line of kids sitting behind them most likely staring at their demise. Alan looks behind,

"I DID NOT SAY YOU COULD LOOK AWAY FROM THE WALL, DID I".

still shouting,

"no" he replies,

"NO WHAT" she shouted,

"No miss"

"GET OVER HERE"

with his trousers down to his ankles, Alan is struggling to get over. He grabs the waist band of his trousers to pull them up so he could walk,

" LEAVE THEM" she shouted,

he gets closer to her, and in almost lighting speed, she pulls his under pants down and pulls him over her knee. Within moments he's screaming out in pain. He knows it isn't her hand pounding his exposed behind, whilst she is pushing his hand away as he attempts to defend himself. It felt smaller than the palm of her hand. It was only after several blows, when she pulls him up, and seeing a hair-brush with a flat back in her hand. He's still wailing from the pain. She pulls his underpants up then sends him to join the others on the bench ordering Frank over to her. He did nothing to warrant a beating, but still gets the same as what Alan got.

It's mid June and the school kids break up for the summer holidays. Most of them go away for a week, split into two groups, so one group goes one week, another the week following when the first group returns. Peter is amongst them. Alan is still young and stays at the home with his other friends from his age group, occasionally going to Queen's Park, or the Transport museum nearby. But mostly in the back garden unless the weather is bad, in which case he has to go in the play hall where Barbara seems always to be. Alan is running around the garden waving his arms around like a lunatic because he still has memories of the time he got stung and is panicking trying to wave off the wasp that's chasing him. Probably to the amusement of the others.

Chapter 9
Karma

Summer holidays are finally over and School is about to start in two days' time. Alan is finally looking forward to his first day at school, but then that same night, Saturday, he suddenly feels sick. He tells Moreen he has a stomach pain.

"how bad does it feel" she asks,

he's almost in tears,

"it's really bad" he replies,

"come on, let's see if we can get you something for it"

she says as she gently takes his hand and slowly walks him up to the office. He's struggling to walk and crouches down a few times as Moreen helps him up each time going at his pace. As he gets to the office door, Barbara walks out,

"what's wrong with him".

she asks, in a condescending manner. Moreen explains.

"he has a stomachache".

she walks in front of him and puts her hand on his forehead.

"there's nothing wrong with him she says".

Just then the contents in his stomach erupts like a violent volcano, spewing vomit all over Barbara's overalls. Moreen grabs his arms from the back holding him. As Barbara tries to jump back, she slips in the vomit falling backwards. Alan wants to laugh even though his eyes are partially blur from his tears but can't as a second wave pours from his gut covering her legs. She pushes herself back as the third wave flows out. By the time he's done, a quarter of the landing is covered. Matron has already come out from the office hearing the commotion.

"Moreen, take him and clean him up while I call the doctor" she says,

Barbara is standing there as if in shock and clearly not amused as Moreen and Alan go to the bathroom. Once there, Moreen starts laughing as she takes the vomit-soaked clothes off Alan. He has no idea why as she won't tell him, but he can only guess it has something to do with Barbara. After cleaning him up, she takes him back to the office. The floor outside the office is wet from the mopping up and Barbara has gone. Sometime later the doctor arrives, checks him over and diagnoses him with a stomach bug saying he'll need to rest for a week. Hearing this Alan is disappointed that he'll miss his first day at school. On Sunday he spends the whole day in bed occasionally sneaking over to the window watching his friends play wishing he could join them by now not feeling any of the effects of the pain or sickness from last night. Moreen occasionally checks in on him bringing orange juice as he isn't allowed to eat that day. Monday comes as he still lays in bed still recovering from his bug from the other night watching his friends changing into their new school uniform getting ready for their first day. John has already left the room as usual as he watches the rest dress then leave. Moreen looks back at him,

"I'll come back in a minute",

she says as she walks out leaving the door wide open. A minute turns into nearly an hour as she had to walk the others to School. When she does arrive back, she brings a tray with Alan's breakfast as he's still confined to his bed for another few days. Moreen checks up on him periodically bringing him his meals and slipping in some beverages. Late afternoon his friends come running into the room from school straight over to his bed,

"is it true, is it" all excited jumping while laughing,

Alan is smiling confusingly trying to figure out what they're trying to say. John tells them to shush, then says,

"people are saying you were sick all over Barbara and she fell in it, is it true".

Alan smiles for a bit and confirms it is. They all laugh as Moreen walks in.

"why are you lot not changed yet",

she says as they run to their own beds changing out of their school uniforms into their plain clothes.

"go and play" she tells them after they've changed.

The room empties and Moreen curiously asks Alan why they were laughing. Alan says, "they wanted to know about me being sick all over Barbara".

at that moment she burst out laughing and walks out of the room. Alan stares at the door for a while still listening to her laughter until it fades into the distance. He remains in bed for the rest of the week even though he himself feels perfectly well.

A week later, he's finally ready to start his new school. He's excited. He's heard a lot about this place and was always looking forward to the day he got to go. This was it. He puts on his new school uniform. Grey shirt, tie, grey pullover, grey shorts, grey socks and black shoes. As they leave, he's made to wear a duffle coat despite the warm weather, then walks to school with Moreen holding his hand. As he gets closer to Melville infant school, he begins to get nervous unknown what lays ahead. The gates are in sight, though not fully visible yet. He can see other kids his age walking through the opening in the wall. Girls through one opening. Boys through another. Some older, but most wearing the same. One after another they pile in, it seems like it's just another home but with far more kids. He walks past the first gate reserved for the girls to the second gate which is the boys. The playground is covered in tarmac as he walks across the yard making his way into the Victorian school building. The windows are huge and high. Still with his escort, he makes his way into the classroom finally getting the chance to sit down after the half mile gruelling trek that tired his short by now aching legs. He takes his seat sitting next to Lee, a Chinese boy also starting for the first time. The windows inside are also high. The only thing visible to him is the sky. As the grown ups say their goodbyes, tears and wailing begin from the other kids in the classroom including Lee, even though most of them started a week earlier. Alan is at a loss. What's wrong with these people he thinks to himself. He asks Lee why he's crying,

"my mammy", he says.

Alan doesn't feel the kind of emotion his classmates feel. He has no idea what it's like to have that kind of emotional feeling as he just sits and observes what's happening in front of him. The parents leave. Lee becomes his first school friend and both remain friends until the day he never returns to school less than a year later. He never knew what became of him, though he did make other friends over time but tended to keep more to himself. At times he became confused as he watches kids coming to school hand in hand with the grownups who accompany them, kissing their cheeks as they say goodbye with a smile on both faces. And as they are collected, the same kiss to the cheek with some jumping to be lifted and cuddled. To Alan this is not normal as he wondered why he never received such comfort. Alan enjoyed his time at this school, mostly because he is away from his torturer, Barbara, even though he still gets humiliated in the evenings and weekends, by now knowing he has been singled out, most likely because of her humiliation that night on the landing.

The cold winter months arrive and are the very thing the kids in the home hate. It's not so much that the playroom is big and can easily accommodate all the kids, they just like to be outside. In someways the cold doesn't bother them so much as they are prevented from going out, and only in certain circumstances. i.e., snow, if it clear, bright and dry. Even on fireworks night, the younger kids including Alan are stuck inside watching the fire at the bottom of the garden by the sandpit from the window as the few fireworks that are available are set off. Though in fairness beverages are provided.

It's Christmas time, and all the kids are up and dressed. After Breakfast all are congregated in the entrance hall sitting on the wide stairs as one by one they leave as someone comes to pick them up. The numbers dwindle until only one remains. Alan doesn't know where they've all gone, but he's left alone in the entrance hall. Is someone going to pick him up? He himself doesn't know, but waits assuming someone will just like his friends. Time goes on, he still waits. It's not to be. No one will be taking him. The only person who comes for him is Matron. She takes him into the staff room where there's a TV. For the rest of the day that's where he remains occasionally going into the playroom relieved Barbara for once is not there. He cannot understand why no one would come and take him but alone it felt strange. Later in the evening a few would return, but he felt almost as lonely as he did when he was at Brenda's house earlier in the year. He alone sleeps in his bedroom. His friends gone. The sound of the night is different. The creaking of the central heating pipes sound like they're being tapped on, and an eerie feeling being all alone. Eventually he falls into sleep. When he wakes up the next morning, more are back in their beds, obviously arriving back late night, the rest return throughout the day.

It a new year 1970. Alan is back at school, he's beginning to enjoying his time there making new friends, but mostly glad to be away from Barbara. He despises her. He sees her as picking on him all of the time. With the exception of the humiliations and minor beatings from her before summer, nothing much else happens.

Chapter 10
The First Holiday

It's mid June and schools have broken up for the Summer holiday. Alan along with other kids are on their way to the homes holiday location. Hours of travelling later, they arrive at their destination. The site is Cookswood Deep inside the Scottish forestry of Culzean County Park. There are pine trees everywhere down a dirt path to an opening to the site. Just inside, there's a single storey white cottage that looks like something out of the Robert Louis Stevenson's movie, 'kidnapped' a movie not yet released. Behind the cottage sits two eight berth caravans with one in sight from the cottage driveway. The other hidden behind the cottage. The minibus stops in the driveway then drives off after dropping the occupants off. This is their home for the next week as it's shared throughout the holiday period with all the home's children selected weekly. The girls are in the second caravan with the boys in the first. Barely in the boys are told to sleep. Wishful thinking as they've slept pretty much the entire journey and are too excited to sleep anyway.

"Can we play" one of the boys asks,

"no" replies Joan,

who's one of three staff members assigned to look after the boisterous bunch for the week.

"Miss we already slept in the bus on the way" said Alan,

anxious to get out and explore his surroundings. But she's not having it.

"you'll just have to try and sleep" she replies.

Peter is also on the first week to Alan's delight, and as the home's clown, he decides to make snoring sounds, this followed by others including Alan in between their bouts of laughter.

"If I hear one more sound from you lot, you'll be sitting in here for the rest of the week" Joan says feeling annoyed.

Of course, no one sleeps. Well with the exemption of Jimmy who is snoring for real, though not annoyingly.

An hour later Joan asks if anyone wants hot chocolate. All hands are raised except for Jimmy as he's just coming out of whatever world he was in for the past hour. A little nudge from Alan McKenzie soon gets him up.

"would you like some hot chocolate"

pausing for a few seconds

"its Jimmy right" finishing her sentence.

"yes" Jimmy replies.

A few minutes later the hot chocolate and biscuits are finished,

"off you go, and don't go too far",

Joan tells the excited young holiday makers as they rush out of the caravan. It's Alan first holiday. Although he can't see the sea, he can hear the Seagulls, and the waves beyond the trees. Sand makes up most of the paths around the site. The site itself is grassed. He can't wait to get on the beach and up close to the sea as he's observed the sea almost daily from Blairvadach but has never been on the beach or close to it now anxious to finally get up close to it.

"Miss can we go to the beach" he asks.

"Peter, can I trust you to take them and look after them" she asks,

Peter knows the place as he's been every year. Some of the girls also regulars want to go.

"we'll help to look after them" one says.

"Off you go then, and keep away from the sea" she says,

"ok" comes the reply.

Off they go, though not down the main dirt path which is the quickest way as it leads directly to the beach. Peter chooses to take the path that goes through the woods, which starts a few metres from behind the boys caravan.

"Let's go" Peter says,

"and stay with me" saying it loud enough for the staff to hear.

They walk towards the opening where the path starts at the woods only to be met by a wooden plaque on a pole portraying a pirate's symbol which is clearly a prank from some previous users. Through they go following Peter and the other few regular boys and girls alike. They're a fair distance into the woods now. The caravans and cottage are out of sight. Peter takes them left along an even narrower path heading them down hill but not very steep. The sound of the waves are getting louder and the calm blue ocean can be seen through the woods sparking from the late afternoon sun reflecting off the waves as they pound the golden sandy beach. Alan is taken back by the sight of it as he's only experienced it from a distance and passing in a taxi a year earlier. Now he's just few feet away from standing on the sand filled with excitement. They come to the end of the path with just a few long blades of grass separating them from the Beach. Ships in the far distance fill the picture. Alan finally stands on the beach. His feet sink into the soft sand as he walks, with his shoes taking in sand.

"TAKE YOUR SHOES AND SOCKS OFF, ITS EASIER TO WALK"

Peter shouts. Everyone drops sitting on the soft sand taking their footwear off and leaving them in a neat pile by the woods edge where they've just emerged from. This part of the beach is secluded so there's no risk of their shoes and socks going missing. They go down to the water's edge,

"we were told not to go near the water" Frank said,

"don't worry" Peter says,

as he walks right into the wave. Alan, Frank, Jimmy and

Alan McKenzie, look at each other, smiling as most of the others wade through the water. They know they will be defying an instruction if they follow the already lawless bunch having fun in front of their eyes. Alan McKenzie takes the lead, inching his way towards the water. The rest cautiously follow, while Alan constantly looks back into the woods to see if they're being watch.

"come on" Alan McKenzie says nervously,

as they watch him put his foot in the water and quickly take it out.

"OOO ITS COLD" he shouts,

then wades back in. The rest follow almost mimicking Alan McKenzie's first attempt with the exception of Alan already put off by Alan McKenzie's reaction to the cold water. This carries on for a while until they get a bit bored. Alan avoided going in, not because he was told not to, but he just thought it would be cold from the actions of his friends and sat further up on the dry sand just watching the others having fun. peter takes the lead coming out of the water,

"come on".

he says using the evening sun as a watch to say,

"it's time to go back".

With that, splashes of sea water flies around the feet of the kids running in from the sea. Alan watches on as the sun from behind them shines through the clear droplets of water sparkling with it splashing up behind them causing an incredible sight to look at. Then as they hit the sand, it too flies in the air as they take each step running up toward their socks and shoes, sitting by them dusting the sand off their feet already dried from the sand soaking up most of the water.

"Right, stick with me".

Peter says as they make their way back up the narrow path leading to the site.

Joan looks at them as they arrive back to the site standing semi-circle with the other two staff member chatting as they do waiting for them to get a little closer,

"did you enjoy yourselves" she asks,

"yes" Peter Replies,

"what did you do" she asks,

"erm we played in the sand, built sandcastles and that" Peter says,

"sandcastles" Joan asks with a confused tone,

"yes" he replies.

Joan is bobbing her upper torso side to side as if to see if they are hiding anything behind them.

"what did you build sandcastles with",

she asks raising her eye browse knowing full well they

have nothing. Peter looks around realising he's slipped up.

"Alan" she says,

"I want you to tell me the truth".

giving him a stern look,

"did you go into the sea",

she asks still with that stern look looking straight into his eyes.

"no" he replies,

"are you telling me the truth" she asks,

"yes" he replies,

"ok go and wash your hands",

she tells the group of youngsters as she walks into the caravan to prepare dinner. Night has arrived and everyone goes to bed at the same time even though it's still light outside as the days are at their longest few weeks. Still excited they barely sleep the first night constantly being told off by Joan for the noise and giggling. Next morning they're up early. The site is not huge but more than spacious to run around. Alan chooses to sit on the caravan tow hitch as it's partially shaded from the hot early morning June sun just watching the others play. It's already hot and he's not too keen on the hot sun. Joan comes out from the caravan and walks over to him,

"Alan do you want serial" she asks,

"yes please" he replies,

with two boxes in her hand she asks

"which would you like, Cornflakes or rice crispies".

"that one please" pointing to the rice crispies.

He can hear the serial being poured into a bowl with the windows and door open allowing the air to flow through the caravan to cool it down. She returns with two bowls handing one to Alan and one for herself. She sits on the camping chair next to Alan.

"last night when I asked you if you went into the sea" She tells him,

"I Didn't" he replies,

"I know you didn't. We were watching through the woods" she said,

pausing then carrying on,

"I Asked you because if I asked the others they would have lied. We knew you and Frank didn't go in"

Alan looks at her confused, he knows Frank did go in but wasn't going to grass him up, though for a while he's trying to get his head around why she's telling him this. Then says, "miss, I don't understand".

"what do you think would happen if I asked the others" she asked,

"I don't know" he replies,

"they would have lied, then I would have to tell them we were watching. What do you think would happen then" she asks.

"they would be in trouble" he replies,

"of course," she says,

"what they did was wrong, but I did not want to ruin your first day," she says,

"ohh ok" he replies,

still unsure why she's telling him.

Most of the week is pretty much like any other day with a similar routine. Walks through the woods and around the area. Quiet and pleasant even for young minds, and not at all boring as the area itself is huge and goes on for miles. The exploration is something that did keep them busy. The week felt quick and the minibus turns up to collect the children. Off they go on their way back to the home again sleeping most of the journey as they did on their arrival. By the time they arrive back, it's straight into the dining room for dinner as its already late, soon after, they're all upstairs and and straight into the bath. After spending the entire week with no shower or bathing facilities on site apart from a wash basin for face wash and brushing teeth. It was a luxury they lacked, but they didn't care, it was the best week he ever had. As night came they're back in their own beds, and unlike most nights, they are almost out as soon as their tired heads hit the pillow.

Chapter 11
The Second Name Change

Next morning the kids are back to their usual routine. Get up go down for breakfast, then outside. There are bags in the hall most likely waiting to be loaded on to the minibus for the next group to go for their holiday. After a week away things feel different even though it's as it was before they left. The holiday did achieve one thing, and that was bringing the group closer together. They spent more time as a group which seemed to be the trend with all after their return. There is nothing different on their return with the exception that there are three new boys at the home, all brothers. The youngest joins Alan's group while the other two join the older group. He's sat alone on the little steps that lead to the hard surface up the little hill while Alan and the others are playing. He grabs Alan's attention as he looks on. Alan notices him sat on the steps looking upset and starts to walk over,

"where are you going" Jimmy asks,

"Over there" Alan replies,

Pointing and walking over to the new boy. He can see tears as he gets closer to him,

"what's wrong, why are you crying" Alan asks,

"I want my brothers" he replies,

"where are they" Alan asks,

"they went with the others to the park" he says while still

crying,

"what your name" Alan asks,

"Alan" he replies,

"no your name"

"Alan" he reply's again,

"Your name is Alan" Alan asks,

"yes" he replies.

"really"

"yes"

"that's my name too" Alan tells him,

he looks up at him, then smiles.

"We both have the same name then" New Alan asks,

"yes" Alan says then carrying on to say,

"you see that boy over there",

pointing to Alan McKenzie chasing his other friends,

"which one" he asks,

"the tall one chasing Jimmy, the shorter boy".

"aye" he says,

"his name is Alan too".

he looks over then back to Alan,

"is it" he asks,

"yes" Alan says

New Alan giggles, and they get talking for a while. Alan McKenzie calls Alan to join them to play. Alan turns to New Alan and says

"Do you want to play with us",

"aye" he replies,

then spending the rest of the day with them. As evening approaches, new Alan is reunited with his brothers Tom and Archie. New Alan introduces Alan to his brothers expressing amusement at the name. In normal circumstances the younger kids are separated from the older kids, but new Alan is allowed to sleep in the same room as his brothers. They have most of the bedroom to themselves as most of the others have gone to the caravan with just a couple including Peter left. The next morning Alan is taken to the office by Moreen. She makes no comment but to say,

"Matron needs to talk to you".

His first thought is he's obviously done something and about to be punished, but Moreen seems to be upbeat, joking and happy. He knows enough in the past year being around Moreen that she's caring and wouldn't be in that mood if he was in trouble, which gives him some comfort. The office door is already open as they approach. Matron has acknowledged their arrival by her quick glance before looking into her papers again. Still as they arrive at the door, Moreen knocks then enters.

"shall I shut the door" Moreen asks,

causing Alan to look up nervously thinking,

"maybe I am in trouble".

"no, it's fine" Matron replies,

Still with her head down writing, though not much comfort for Alan now. She stops writing, looks up, then looks over to Alan with a smile,

"I hear you've made friends with Alan the new boy who arrived a couple of days ago" she says,

Suggesting he arrived while they were at the caravan.

"yes" Alan replies,

"and you're also friends with Alan McKenzie" she adds.

"yes Miss" he replies confusingly.

"Moreen has told us it's causing a problem with three of you having the same name when you're all together" she says,

Alan replies by shrugging his shoulders not able to say anything,

"your records show your name is Alan Derek, did you know that" She asks,

Alan replies with a nod to say yes,

"to avoid any confusion, as of today we're calling you Derek, just Derek as no one else has that name and it's easier for everyone. All the staff have been told this. Are you ok with this"?

Alan looks at Moreen, she nods, he looks back a Matron shrugging his shoulders replying,

"yes"

"good, you can go now Derek".

he smirks as he walks away trying to figure out what just happened fully unaware that change is about to create chaos for the rest of that week.

He joins his friends outside. Now already completely forgotten about the discussion that happened five minutes ago. As the week goes on, one of the days become a painful reminder of what happens when he forgets his name change. The weather is fine in the morning as they play in the garden. After lunch they play outside again. Derek is still being addressed as Alan by his friends still completely forgetting it's been changed despite Moreen addressing him by his new name. As the afternoon goes on, the weather changes. It becomes dull. It's not cold but wet with fine particles of rain and wind. The younger group are told to go into in the playroom the oldest group still away at the caravan and the remaining older boys at the local park. The person looking after the younger group is as usual Barbara. She's sitting on the bench busy reading her book or knitting. The rest are playing as normal, though noisy. Derek has a fallout with Frank. They're arguing and Derek tells him to get lost loud enough to catch Barbara's attention,

"DEREK GET OVER HERE" she shouts,

everyone stops looks around including Derek,

"I WON'T TELL YOU AGAIN"

she says looking directly over at Derek. He's confused because he's completely forgotten it's him. He looks behind him thinking it's not him. The others think she's crazy, and they too look around wondering who Derek is. They have no idea Alan is now Derek. By now Barbara is fuming. She gets off the bench speed walking to Derek, grabs his arm and marches him to the front,

"when I tell you to do something, you do it"

she says as she sits down on the bench pulling his trousers and underwear down then pulling him over her knee pounding his backside. He's screaming in pain. Alan McKenzie shouts

"HE DID NOTHING WRONG, WHY ARE YOU HITTING HIM"

"YOU WATCH YOUR LIP" she reply's,

"WHATS HE DONE" he says,

"YOU, GET DOWN HERE NOW" she orders him,

then stops the beating pulling Derek up still with no explanation about the name change. Derek attempts to pull his pants up, but she stops him and orders him to stand facing the wall,

"I've not finished with you yet",

she tells him, then orders the rest to sit on the benches. She repeats the same beating to Alan McKenzie though he gets to keep his underwear on, then orders him to stand next to Derek still with his trousers down. Whilst Derek is waiting for his second beating, Barbara tells one of the girls to get a bar of soap from the girls toilets directly across from the playroom. Alan McKenzie whispers to Derek saying,

"she's a bitch" then sniggers,

causing Derek to laugh. The soap is brought in,

"you think this is funny".

she says as she walks over, slapping Alan McKenzie on his backside before grabbing Derek back over.

"This is what we do to naughty children who use bad words",

she says as she tries to force the soap into Derek's mouth. He resists keeping his mouth tightly closed. She pinches his nose causing him to open his mouth to gasp for air, giving her the chance to push the soap into his mouth with his teeth acting like a cheese grater peeling layers of soap into his mouth. He doesn't know what she refers to as a bad word. He's never sworn and has to that day never heard a bad word being said. She stops, pulls him up and orders him back to where Alan McKenzie stands. After a while, she tells him to pull his pants up telling the rest to carry on playing. Later that afternoon, the rain stops and the sun returns. Barbara goes to the window by the door leading to the garden. She looks out then tells the kids they can go out to play. Once out, Derek, Alan McKenzie, and new Alan stick together. Derek still spitting soap taste out from his earlier experience, asked Alan McKenzie,

"what does bitch mean" both Alan's laugh,

"you don't know what bitch means" he replies,

"no"

Alan tries to explain, though it would be some years later before Derek finds out a bitch has nothing to do with a cow. Shortly after school restarts. He's at the same infant's school but in a different classroom and still with his classmates from the previous year. He's still enjoying his time there, though struggles with his writing and maths. He clearly understands everything being said but struggles to put it on paper.

Chapter 12
The Christmas Angel

Christmas arrives and everyone is excited with the decorations up. On the stairs windowsill a decoration is set up. A cotton wool base with a pine tree with Santa and sleigh figures placed on it. A few days before Christmas it disappears. There's a hunt for it and everyone is questioned about its disappearance and if anyone saw it. No one owns up and a search is ordered with everyone's rooms being searched. Derek stands by his bed as the search comes to his room standing next to the wardrobe.

"have you got it" Moreen asks,

"no" he replies, nervously,

"let's have a look".

she says as she grabs the handle opening the cupboard door then pausing. She looks at Derek then closes the door.

"right, you can leave now"

she says casually as if nothing's happened holding onto Derek's shoulder. The rest leave then she opens it again. There it is, sitting at the bottom of the wardrobe laid out exactly as it was on the windowsill.

"why did you take it" she asks,

"I wanted to decorate the cupboard" he replies.

She closes the door and gives him a lecture about how wrong it is to take something that doesn't belong to him. He sits there teary eyed knowing he's done wrong but can't respond.

"We'll say nothing about this. I know you didn't mean to take it" she says, before telling him to go.

As night-time arrives he makes his way up stairs and notices the decoration has been place back to its original place. As he gets to the second part of the staircase, Moreen is standing there at the top. Derek looks at her then looks back at the window where it sits before looking back at Moreen. She gives him a smile raising her eyebrows. He knows he got away with it and thanks her. He makes his way into the bedroom walking towards the wardrobe to get his pyjamas out. As he opens the wardrobe door, he notices a sparkle coming from half way down. He looks and sees decorative foil hanging in the wardrobe with a sheet of cotton wool laid out at the bottom. He takes his pyjamas out with a huge smile on his face and as he closes the cupboard door right there standing by the room door is Moreen, herself with a huge smile. It's at that moment he understood why those kids at his school were so attached to their parents he finally understood that love is powerful it's a strange feeling. He's five years old, nearly six, and standing before him a woman totally unrelated to him by blood. But still he feels it. He wants to walk over and hug her but feels shy. He puts his pyjamas on and climbs into bed. Moreen is now inside the room checking everyone is in bed tucking them in one by one. She goes to Derek last. He still has thoughts of wanting to hug her just like he's observed other kids do at school, but shyness gets the better of him. Instead, he looks at her, she looks back smiling.

Then as she's tucking him in, in a faint voice, she asks,

"do you like it"

Shy from his thoughts, he smiles and nods to say yes. She leaves the room as usual leaving the door slightly ajar.

Christmas Eve comes and everyone is called to the entrance hall. All are told to sit on the stairs.

As Santa arrives he hands each a present. One to each child then later they are sent to bed. On Christmas Day everyone wakes up to find a stocking filled with chocolate bars at the foot of their beds. They get up, have breakfast, then told to change into their best clothes. When they're done, all are congregated into the main entrance hall just like they did last year. As each are collected by what Derek now knows their relatives. Parents, uncles, aunts, they leave the home for one or two days over Christmas. Derek again stands staring at the large clock in the main hall wondering if anyone would ever come for him. He knew they wouldn't, but still hoped as he stood silently just listening. Tick tock the huge clock sounds in the now empty hall with the odd voices being heard from the remaining staff members with a bag sat on the sideboard near the main door. It felt like hours staring at the clock, there's a noise coming from the main door as it creeks in the wind. He hears footsteps coming down from the top part of the stairs hidden by the platform at the foot of the large window overlooking the bag garden, Matron appears on the platform. He's resigned to the fact this is going to be a repeat of last year and he'll be stuck with her playing games. But as she starts to make her way down the main staircase, at that same moment he's distracted by the dining room doorknob turning. He looks back to see Moreen emerging from the dining room with his coat.

"put this on",

she says, as she hands it over to him. She's already wearing hers.

"How would you like to stay with me for tonight" she says,

a huge smile appears on his face.

"yes please" he replies,

"come on then" she says,

he looks over to Matron just stepping off the bottom step, she smiles.

"off you go and enjoy yourself" she says,

he turns back to Moreen as she picks the bag up from the sideboard.

"come on"

she says opening and holding the door open for him to walk out. She takes him to her house. There's no time to get to know his surroundings as Moreen's keen to get out fast. They have drinks and biscuits then head out to Glasgow city centre by bus which is the only mode of transport running that day. It's his first visits to a funfair and a completely new experience for him. He goes on the rides, eats ice cream, goes to the cafe for lunch, even though it's fish and chips. Her attitude outside the home is completely different to how it is in the home. Even though he loved her for the way she treated him at the home, this is different. He sees other families and how they are interacting, seeing no difference to how both he and she are interacting. He has a feeling of security finally and there's no dogs to attack him. It's the best time he's ever had even though it's cold. They leave the fair and walk through the square where loudspeakers blast Christmas songs and carols surrounded by decorations, colourful lights and a huge Christmas tree which is the central attraction. They go back to her house where he watches TV in black and white. Even though the home has one, it's never appealed to him as there is plenty to do without the need to watch any. Moreen spends her time in the kitchen occasionally peeping into the living room to check up on him. He knows this because she has no carpets in the house apart from a large rug in the living room and her footsteps are obvious. He can smell the food from where he sits. As he continues to watch TV she calls him into the kitchen. A kitchen not that much bigger than that of Brenda's from almost two years earlier, even the layout is almost identical. He sits at the table where she waits,

"have you forgotten something" she asks smiling at him.

he looks around looking at her still smiling, then says.

"no"

"did you wash your hands" she asked,

he looks at her and smiles, then gets up without a word

walking over to wash his hands in the kitchen sink.

"I'll let this one go, but kitchen sinks are not for washing hand in" she tells him,

"sorry"

he replies as they tuck into the sliced-up roast turkey. After dinner they both sit watching TV until It's bedtime. Unlike Brenda's house, Moreen's is warm and more comfortable. Moreen tucks him in as she's done many times. He looks around the room. It's bigger than the bedroom at Brenda's with the curtains closed. The room smells fresh but empty. When all is done, she says,

"goodnight",

he sleeps well then gets up for breakfast in the morning,

"ah, there's no milk" Moreen says as she opens the fridge.

"I'll just pop over to the shop, it's just across the road" she says pointing to the front door,

"can I go" Derek asks,

"are you sure you want to go", she replies.

"Yes"

"ok, put your slippers on" she says,

"they're already on" he replies,

She writes a list and gives it to him along with money. He takes his time looking at it. It's the first time he's ever handled money,

"come on" she says,

his eyes are still fixated to the money as he walks out the opened front door.

"I'll wait here for you"

she says as he walks down the steps leading to the road still in his Pyjamas and dressing gown. The shop is just across the road in sight of the house. The road is quiet with no traffic with it being Boxing Day. He runs across the road into the shop and hands the note over to the shop keeper.

"are you staying at Moreen's"

The shopkeeper asks looking out the window to where she's standing,

"yes" he replies,

"you must be the wee boy from the home" he says,

"aye" he replies,

"she talks about you a lot. She likes you" he says,

Derek looks at him then looks out the window to where Moreen stands. The shop keeper fills the bag and takes the money handing him the change.

Again his eyes are fixated on the coppers and silver as he picks each coin, investigating them.

"here, take this",

The shopkeeper says as he hands him chocolate with the shopping bag,

"a wee Christmas present from me" he says,

"and don't run with that bag, it has glass bottles in it",

"thank you",

he says as he walks out of the shop with the heavy bag, this time walking.

After breakfast, they play board games for the rest of the morning before leaving back for the home after Lunch. As they make their way back, Moreen is talking to Derek asking if he liked staying there. His thoughts were for that night,

"yes" he says,

It did not occur to him that she was talking long term, but it will be a few years later when he would find out she was trying to adopt him.

Chapter 13
Barbara's Revenge

A year has passed. Derek is now six years old and it's a new decade. It's 1971 and spring is now in full bloom. Back at school they get to use scissors as part of an activity for that day. Whilst doing the activity, Derek wants to see how well the scissors cut. He tries to cut his eyebrows with success. He knows it's a lot as the evidence is right there in front of him. As the teacher comes over he's preparing for the worst. Thoughts are running through his head like, what will she do? Will it be the ruler, or will she have a hairbrush? Will she use her hand? With the constant encounters with Barbara, he's become paranoid as he expects punishment for even the most minor thing. She does have a ruler in her hand, so his nerves gets the better of him. He tries to think of ways to get out of this predicament. What excuses can I make, he thinks to himself. She's getting closer then stops right in front of him. This is it he thought, but to his surprise she looks at him, smiles and says,

"what have you done".

in a softly spoken tone. She takes the weapon from his hand and says,

"we'll say it was an accident".

The relief from her comments allows him to relax, realising he's free and begins to like his teacher. Moreen collects him and the others from School as she's done since he started. The teacher tells her about his little incident seeing the funny side of it. Moreen jokes about it saying,

"I may need to draw eyebrows on there".

They arrive back at the home going through the far door that leads to the cloakroom. Moreen leaves them to hang their coats up. As they're about to leave the cloakroom, Barbara notices the mess on his eyebrows. He realises his relief from punishment is short lived as he's dragged into the playroom and ordered to drop his pants. He knows what's coming and refuses. The others have gone to change. With no other person there she tries to pull his shorts down. Derek is resisting knowing what she is going to do. She grabs the waist of his shorts trying to force them down, shouting at him using words he's never heard before, then slaps him on the face causing him to raise his hands to protect himself, thus giving her the chance to pull them down, then she forcefully pulls him over her knee subjecting him to repeated beatings with her hairbrush. Barbara has finally got her revenge. Derek knows it but is powerless to stop it. Whack after whack with no rest. She's clearly enjoying it whilst in a rage shouting at Derek as she pounds him on his bare end. He is in too much pain to hear what she's saying. Even at the age of six, Derek knew this is wrong and isn't right. He's screaming in pain. At some point during this he hears a loud voice.

"WHAT ON EARTH DO YOU THINK YOU ARE DOING",

a familiar voice he instantly recognises. The shouts are coming from behind him where the door is. The beating stops abruptly as Derek looks back. Standing by the door with a furious look on her face is Moreen. Barbara pushes Derek from her knees causing him to roll onto the floor as Moreen orders her to leave the room. Moreen walks over towards him, stops and says,

"you'll be ok now",

She crouches down in front of him helping him to his feet and pulls his pants and shorts up. She sits him on the newly installed side box's which keeps the toys and apparatus in then comforts him. After calming him down and consoling him, she takes him up to his bedroom still shaken from the beating. His friends are already outside playing.

"Derek, change your clothes and wait here till I come back" Moreen tells him,

She leaves the room as he undresses. As he's getting into his plain clothes he hears shouting. He goes to the door and opens it. The shouting is coming from the office at the far end of the landing. The office door is closed and there's an argument going on. He struggles to understand what's being said but clearly hears the voices of both Moreen and Barbara. He hears his name mentioned then goes back into the room closing the door and walking over to the window still hearing the now muffled shouting. He looks out the window watching the rest of the kids playing, particularly watching his friends. He hears the office door slam and fast heavy footsteps from heavy heals heading towards his room. He knows it's Barbara because that's what she wears. His heart starts beating fast as the footsteps get closer. Then just as he thought the door is going to open, he hears them going downstairs. At that moment with a sigh of relief both Moreen and Matron walk into the room. Matron stops by the door as Moreen walks over and asks Derek to take his trousers and underwear down. He looks at Matron.

"it's ok Matron just want to see the marks" she says,

he complies not able to see them for himself.

"Ok" Matron says after looking.

"you can pull them back up" Moreen tells him.

Matron leaves then Moreen tells him to stay in the room for now as she leaves. Derek goes back to the window watching his friends and waiting. After a while Moreen returns.

"are you ok now" she asks,

"yes" he replies,

"if you want to stay here you can, otherwise you can go out and play but it will be teatime soon" she says,

he points out the window saying,

"can I go out".

"yes" she replies as she escorts him to the stairs.

That is the last time he sees Barbara at the home. He was never told what became of her.

Chapter 14
Hot Summer

The Summer days are leading up to his last days at infant school. There are work men at the school measuring up for a new block. Derek is fascinated by the measuring tape they're using. At break time he bugs them with silly questions only a six-year-old would ask as they let him measure and show him how it works. Others join in and soon a crowd is forming with everyone wanting to try this huge real tape. At home time Moreen stands by the gate waiting to walk the children back to the home. As they walk past the row of houses, they come across one with a small garden with flowers neatly arranged. Moreen leans over the garden wall, takes a Rose and hands it to Derek. As they walk up the road within minutes of receiving the rose, he feels a sharp pain on his backside followed by a hand coming from behind grabbing the rose. The lady who owns the house from where the flower was taken is furious, but Derek being small would bear the brunt of Moreen's kindly mistake. It's not hard to see why this woman would not take it out on Moreen. She's tall and big in size and mean looking. The kind of person at sight you would not want to mess with. But anyone who knows her, knows she's kind-hearted and caring. Clearly, she had forgotten in that moment in time the lecture she gave Derek just a few months before about not taking things that don't belonging to you, though it didn't even cross his mind at the time.

Schools out and as they did last year they go on holiday to the same location at Culzean. There's a few different faces this time but also a bit boring without Peter. He always kept them entertained with his Gilamashina stories and antics, though still, there's plenty to do. Back at the home after the weeks holiday they spend most of the summer in the Garden. It's a hot and dry year, and most are getting sunburnt, including Derek. Temperatures are flaring. Arguments and fights are taking place which is totally out of character for most. That night an argument breaks out between Derek and Frank and they get into a fight. Derek is being overpowered and bites Frank's hand, he screams and Moreen runs in running straight over to them breaking the fight up.

"stop it the pair of you" she says,

"he started it".

"no, he started it" both arguing.

"stop" she says again,

"look what he did",

Frank says showing the teeth marks on his hand still crying. Moreen looks at Derek and says,

"did you do that. Did you bite him".

"aye" he replies,

"excuse me" she says,

"yes" he replies again.

She grabs his arm and slaps his behind.

"you don't bite people" she says,

this is the first time she's ever hit Derek. He looks at her.

"I had to do this, you needed to be punished for hurting him" she says.

tears are starting the fall from Derek's eyes not because of any pain. She didn't hit him hard enough to cause pain. But because he felt hurt inside that she hit him,

"why did you do it" she asked,

he turned his head to Frank who's still crying, and looks at him for a bit.

"I'm waiting" she says,

he looks back at her and says,

"I was punishing him".

she rolls her eyes trying hard not to laugh with little success. Derek looks at Frank, he too starts laughing causing Derek and the others to laugh.

"It's not funny",

Moreen says trying to control her own laughter.

"apologise to him" she says,

"why, he started it" he says,

"I don't care who started it, you bit him so apologise".

He looks at Frank who's smiling now and pauses before saying

"sorry"

"I'm sorry too",

Frank says without any prompting. He looks at Moreen whose smiling giving her approval with a nod.

As the summer comes to an end, they're moved to another room at the front of the home. It's a much bigger room with older kids including his new friend Alan. Moreen is no longer looking after him, he'll have new staff members looking after him from now on. There are no goodbyes as they will still see each other on a daily basis. Just days before the end of the Summer holidays, Derek sneaks out the front by the side door with Peter. They see one of the staff members walking up the driveway and hide in the shrubs as she walks past them. She drops her cigarette not stamping it out. As soon as she walks through the side door, Peter quickly runs from the shrubs and picks it up. There's not much left. He takes a drag from it then passes it on to Derek. He's never tried smoking before, so rather than taking the smoke in, he's blowing into it. Peter shows him how it's done. He takes it following his instructions. After taking a drag from it he coughs for a good while. His eyes are watering as he coughs. That was it for him. No more, however Peter carries on then out of the blue he asks Derek a question.

"Where's your mum and dad".

Derek stands there looking at him for a while. This is a question no one has ever asked him before and something he's never thought about. With being brought up in care his entire life to this point, he's never had any thoughts of having parent. Who they are, what they are, what purpose do they have, or have any feeling towards what would be considered natural for kids his age. After thinking for a while, the only answer he comes out with is,

"they're dead".

Peter asks,

"How did they die".

"I don't know" he responds,

"did you ever see them".

again, he thinks for a while before replying,

"no",

Now desperately hoping he won't keep asking questions about his parents simply because he never knew them, or what they looked like, what they did, or why they're dead. He didn't ask anymore but within moments both are distracted by the side door opening and the same staff member who walked in moments ago coming out. She stops and looks around.

"I know you're in there, come out" she says,

Derek and Peter look at each other wondering how she

knew. As scared as they both are, they comply and walk out. She stands there in front of them with her hands on her hip fingertips facing back. Something Derek hasn't seen anyone do before.

"where is it" she asks,

both look at each other,

"where's the cigarette" she asks again,

"what cigarette" Peter replies,

"the cigarette I threw down here",

she says pointing to the path,

"we didn't see anything there" Peter says,

she looks at them, then glances around the ground before saying

"you shouldn't be out here, go back in".

then escorts them both back in.

Chapter 15
Humiliation

A new School year is starting and Derek gets ready for his firsts day starting at his new school. The uniform is the same as the one he wore at his last school, just a different tie. There are no adults waiting to take him to school as the School is just around the corner from the home. He's now old enough to go with his friends, some of whom are also starting there the same day. He walks up the road sliding his fingers along the sandstone wall not realising he is scraping the skin off the tip of his fingers. When he reaches the corner to cross the road he notices the redness on his fingertips. It's sore but not to the extent of discomfort. He reaches the corner of his new School and like his infant school, the playgrounds at Pollockshields Primary school are separated for boys and girls. He has to walk past the screaming girls playground to get to the shouting boys playground. He can see the boys in the playground through the railings as he makes his way to the gate on the side street. He's overwhelmed by the number of boys in the playground though there are some boys from each age group from the home, so he is amongst some he knows. The bell goes off and each line up in the playground into their class. Derek along with the other new boys line up on the end just by guessing. With it being the first day back after the holidays, every class is escorted by one teacher as is being repeated on the girls' side. His class is on the first floor where the boys and girls meet up for the first time. As soon as they walk into the classroom they are met by a teacher who turns out to be strict. Derek is already having memories of Barbara,

"how could this be happening" he thinks to himself.

He's not enjoying his first day at all. And matters were only going to get worst. Unlike his last school, there's no craft base learning, this is all book based. His first book has to be covered with brown paper then it's straight into maths, not what he expected. He knows he struggles with words and numbers, and can't understand why, though he doesn't seem to have any problems reading from the blackboard.

The bell rings for break time giving him some relief. They all go outside and Derek is desperate to use the toilet. There are toilets both outside and in. He goes to the outside toilets but is pushed back by the older boys. He's getting desperate almost dancing around. Finally, he gets in. He stops at the door and turns back. The smell of urine fills the entire toilet block. He can't stand the smell and decides to use the toilets just outside his classroom. He goes in and starts making his way upstairs only to be startled by the sudden ringing of the bell just above his head as he's making his way up. Still desperate he stops for a bit as he almost looses control from the sudden blast. He slowly makes his way up. As he gets close to the top he starts wondering why none of the kids are coming up. Finally, he reaches the toilet door. As he's about to walk in, his teacher comes out of the classroom.

"where are you going" she asks,

"toilet" he replies,

"you're supposed to use the outside toilets at break time" she says, "it smells" he replies,

"well, that's no my problem"

she says as she puts her hand on his head and turns it towards the stairs,

"you're supposed to be in assembly",

she tells him as she points to the stairs,

"come on, move it" she says,

"but miss, I need a wee" he says holding his crotch,

"you'll just have to wait" she says,

She starts escorting him back down the stairs he's only just struggled to get up, then along the corridor to the gym hall which triples as the gym hall, dining hall and assembly hall. He enters to the sound of the headmaster shouting at three boys standing against the side wall,

"ahh, another one" he says

as he looks directly at Derek as soon as he walks in.

"Where have you been" he asks,

His teacher intervenes,

"I found him in the toilets upstairs" she says,

Derek looks at her knowing she is lying, but both too

scared and too shy to speak out.

"Come on, get over here and join them",

he says pointing to the three boys against the wall. He walks over looking around feeling embarrassed as all eyes are on him. He gets to the wall and stands between the table and the last boy turning his sideways up to look at them. All of them are a lot bigger than him. By now he is so desperate he fears he might not make it to the toilet. The headmaster is still shouting. By now Derek is only interested in using everything he has to hold it back completely oblivious to the shouting until the headmaster's tawse slams onto the table right next to him making him jump. At that moment he completely looses control. He feels the wee running down his bare legs into his socks and shoes. He dares not look down terrified this could get worse now feeling the pressure and heat in his face from the embarrassment. He hadn't forgotten the severity of what he got for cutting his eyebrows. He knows this is worse and the sound of the strap was clearly going to hurt a hell of a lot more than a hairbrush. The headmaster makes his way to the front finishing the assembly. The boys are told to rejoin their class as they start to make their way back to their classrooms. When they get to the top of the stairs, the teacher stops Derek before he enters the classroom.

"you can go to the toilet now" she says,

he looks at her, then looked down at his crotch. His shorts are dry.

"err ok" he replies confusingly.

He goes into the toilets completely bewildered wondering why his shorts are dry even though he still feels wet. He goes into the cubicle and drops his shorts, they're still wet inside as is his under pants. He realises the white nylon inner part of the shorts that make them a lot thicker prevented it from soaking through. That's why nobody said anything he thought, though it did smell mildly. He cleans himself as much as he can before returning to class.

At lunchtime he goes home for lunch as it's close to the school. As soon as he's eaten, he sneaks upstairs hiding wherever he can when hearing staff and footsteps. He still feels dirty from his earlier experience despite mostly being dry now. He makes his way to the middle bedroom where most of the spare clothes are kept. He remembers this from when he was being sized up for his first school uniform closing the door as he enters. He goes straight to the cupboard where the school uniforms are kept but the door is locked. He tries to force it open but to no avail. As he turns to leave he notices a key in another cupboard down the line. He goes to that one and opens it only to find its full of underwear. He takes the key out hoping it will work. It does and he's in. He hears voices and hides under the bed after closing the cupboard door. No one enters the room and the voices disappeared as they go into the distance. He knows he has to work fast. He gets up and opens the cupboard door searching through the shorts looking for something that might fit. It doesn't dawn on him the sizes are in the shorts themselves. He finds something that looks ok and puts them on the bed then takes his shorts off and looks around to see where he can dump them. No luck so he pushes them down the back of the shelf submerging them hoping they won't be found. He starts putting the new shorts on then realises his underpants still smell even though mildly. He goes to the end cupboard and finds a clean pair repeating what he did with the dirty shorts only this time he's pushing them behind the other underwear. He puts them on realising the shorts are much tighter though not uncomfortably tight. They'll do he thought as he sneaks back out making his way back to school. In hindsight the tighter shorts became a lifesaver for him endless times as his teacher had a habit of pulling the leg of the boys shorts up to spank them. He was saved from this as they are too tight for her to pull up though still, he wasn't saved from the spanking, it just didn't hurt as much as it hurt his classmates.

Halloween arrives and the teacher decides they should make masks for art. Paired up they blow balloons up and start pasting newspaper over it, then left overnight to dry, then bursting the balloon leaving the paper mache. It's then cut in half and each partner creates their own mask, which is the kind of subjects Derek enjoys most and a relief from the torturous reading and writing he struggles with.

Chapter 16
The Old Fool

It the time of year most of the kids look forward to as Christmas comes again and as usual it's pretty much a repeat of the previous years, only this time without Derek borrowing the homes Christmas decorations. And again as with last year, everyone is taken by their relatives with Derek like last year stuck on his own. He doesn't think Moreen will be taking him this year as she no longer looking after his age group, but then to his surprised she appears in front of him and asks him if he's ready. He looks at her and says,

"am I staying with you again".

"of course," she says,

His face lights up and they leave even though he's not staying overnight. But he doesn't know that yet, and unlike last year, this time she's taking him to her parents flat which is one of a few high-rise buildings just on the outskirts of Glasgow city centre. He gets in the front door looking for the stairs, as they bypass the door that leads to the them.

"How do we get up stairs" Derek asks

"We're going up in the lift" she replies.

"What's a lift" Derek asks.

"You'll see"

Moreen replies giving him a smile. She presses a button that looks like a door bell, and when the doors opens no-one is there, and to make things worse, it doesn't open like a normal door. This door opens sideways, something he's never seen before.

"Come on" she says walking inside.

He follows her in finding it weird how tiny the room is. Within seconds the weird door shuts and he feels a weird sensation going through his body thinking the room is moving.

"What's happening" he says looking worried.

"We're going up" Moreen says still smiling

"How"

Derek asks now holding on to the side bars for dear life beginning to panic.

"It's ok, nothings going to happen"

Moreen says realising how scary it is for him. The room stops moving and becomes still. Soon the weird door opens. He looks out realising he's not in the same place.

"Where are we" he asks.

"Come with me"

She says taking his hand and walking him over to the window opposite the moving room. He has to tiptoe to see out the windows,

"Wow, how did we get up here"

He says stepping back from the window overwhelmed by the long drop down.

"That little room we were in is the lift, it goes up and down throughout this building" she says

He says nothing more as they walk along the corridor to her parents flat.

The door is already open, so they both walk in. He looks ahead to the sight of a huge window almost filling the entire wall. He's overwhelmed by the awesome views as he watches the smoke coming from chimneys from a different perspective from when he was passing them on the road just a few years earlier. The city centre in the distance is partially blocked by the haze from those same chimneys spewing smoke for the Christmas Day warmth as families get together. Moreen's mum has cooked Christmas dinner. Derek sits on the specially prepared table in front of the window. He's more focused on the views outside the window than the hours of hard work that lay in front of him. When dinner is finished Derek sits with Moreen's dad watching a western. Whilst the ladies wash up in the kitchen her dad starts a conversation.

"Derek did you enjoy the dinner" he asks,

"yes" he replies in a shy tone.

her dad looks back towards the kitchen door, then says in

a soft quiet voice,

"Derek, wait here and keep quiet".

putting his finger over his mouth saying,

"Shhhh",

He gets up and walks over to the sideboard constantly looking towards the kitchen whilst the ladies can be heard inside chatting away. He opens the sideboard drawer slowly then takes out two chocolate bars slowly walking back over to the settee. Derek at this point is holding his hand over his mouth trying not to laugh finding it funny an old man sneaking around like a child. He sits back down and tells him.

"when Moreen said you were coming for Christmas dinner, I sneaked these without gran knowing", referring to Moreen's mum.

They both start opening the wrappers and as they take one bite a voice from behind shouts,

"YOU'RE GOING TO MAKE HIM SICK, YOU OLD FOOL, HES JUST HAD HIS DINNER"

startling both. They look round to see It's Moreen's Mum,

"what are you talking about woman. They starve them in those places" he replies,

Derek doesn't know where to look, not knowing if they were having a serious argument or just joking around. At that moment Moreen intervenes,

"he gets fed well there and he's probably eaten all the chocolate he got this morning".

looking over to him asking if he did,

"yes" is his reply,

"honestly, you're like a wee bairn at times".

Moreen's mum tells him. He looks at Derek giving him a childlike shrug and a huge smile. Derek still holding the remaining chocolate bar is looking at Moreen waiting for instructions.

"don't look at her it's yours" her dad says,

Moreen can't hold back. She's trying to be serious, but Derek has already worked out and knows she struggles in that area then she herself starts laughing,

"you're just as bad as him",

Her mum tells her before laughing herself. Moreen tells him to eat it. He doesn't stay overnight this time and returns to the home in the evening. Again spending time on his own with only a few staff members remaining and the odd few kids who returned that night. Moreen left after dropping him off. On Boxing Day, the other kids return in dribs and drabs throughout the day.

It's February 1972. Just days after Derek's birthday, lights begin to shut down for periods of time particularly in the evening during the cold dark evenings of winter. For those few weeks the kids are hurdled into the kitchen as the only light source is in the form of a battery powered florescent light which is dimly lit allowing some light to ease panic amongst a few of the kids. Most seem excited with the power cuts not bothering them. But still made to sit with the others with the only entertainment in the form of out of tune songs from the staff trying their best to incite inclusion with little success. This goes on for a good few weeks before things go back to normal.

That year is also an unusually hot Easter, and on the last day of school before the Easter holidays, a message is sent around the school telling all pupils they're welcome to stay behind and watch a movie being put on by the School projected onto a screen in the gym. Derek along with some of the others including Alan McKenzie, new Alan and his two brothers stay behind to watch it. It's a movie about Jesus. After about 30 minutes into the movie the gym hall begins to empty with all including Derek and the others leaving . Probably not the movie primary school kids were expecting. Derek is also building a bond with new Alan and his brothers. They're both the same age. Peter still remains friends but spends more time with his own age group. Still, they get together for his Gilamashina stories, and during the holidays, he's allowed to go to the park without adults as Alan's brothers are with him. After Easter they're back at school.

Chapter 17
The Hospital Visit

The summer holidays are approaching and at school it's just like any other day with one exception. Derek is feeling uncomfortable. The day goes on despite his discomfort, and as he starts to walking home, he realises he is struggling to take each step. The pain is becoming unbearable as he desperately tries to keep a brave face. Finally, he gets home and heads straight for his bedroom. Still in his school uniform he goes and lies down on his bed. It's not long before Jill walks in and tells him to get changed and go outside like everyone else. He tries to explain he's in pain, but she doesn't listen. So, he has no choice and goes out into the back garden.

Of all the days, one of the staff members decided they should have races. "Its bad enough being in pain just walking. Now they want me to run", he thinks to himself. He tells her he's not feeling well and doesn't want to race. This unfortunately for him falls on deaf ears as he's ordered to take part. Both Jill and Moreen are there but Moreen is at another part of the garden with the younger kids. Derek is desperately hoping she'll look at him knowing she'll come to his aid. But her attention is towards those in her charge. His time is now coming. He gets in line with his competitors as streams of tears are running down his face now in even more pain with wearing tight jeans. He runs at the word go, and within a few feet falls to the ground. He can no longer bare the pain. He is screaming out in agony. One of the staff members goes over to him and asks,

"what's wrong with you",

he replies, "it's soar",

she asked, "what's sore?",

but he is too embarrassed to say. She takes his hand and helps him to his feet.

"If you don't tell me what's wrong I can't help you".

she says. He whispers into her ear too embarrassed to say it out loud,

"Come with me".

She says as she takes his hand walking him to the house, now walking with his legs apart struggling more with the excruciating pain in tight jeans that he's nearly outgrown which are not helping one bit. Getting up the stairs, also doesn't help as he finds it a painful mission. Finally, he makes it to the office. The matron asks him to show her where he is hurting. He drops his pants and the response from her is.

"we need to get him to hospital now"

He's hurriedly changed into smart clothes. To this day he can't understand why, though he's relieved his trousers are now loose. He's rushed into hospital. The doctors examine him and gives him some kind of injection. The reason for his discomfort and pain is a result of his genitals swelling up. The doctor gives him 10p, and asks.

"What will you buy with it".

"A water gun"

he says. The doctor reaches over to a drawer, takes out a syringe and hands it to him.

"Use this" he says.

Derek is baffled,

"What is it".

The doctor takes it from him again, and sucks up water with it squirting it on Derek's face. The doctor and the staff member with him laugh.

"It's better than a water gun".

The doctor says as he hands it back to him. He's given antibiotics and told to rest for a week, only on this occasion he doesn't complain and is glad to be getting out of School for a week.

Chapter 18
Summer Horror

Summer holidays have arrived and Derek and the other kids as always look forward to this moment as every year they go back to the same location for the week. For the last few years they always went on the first week, this time they're going on the second week. Mostly it's the same group, but this year Peter is with them, and some new boy they've not seen before. Derek's happy his old friend Peter, along with both Alans, Frank and Jimmy are on holiday the same week. On the way, the new boy sits opposite Derek. He's quiet and doesn't talk much. Derek is having a laugh with his friends. Suddenly the new boy reaches over putting his hand over Derek's mouth saying.

"shush"

with his finger over his own mouth. The others stop talking and start staring at this strange boy. After a few seconds he lets go and says.

"It's bad manners to talk when you pass a graveyard".

Everyone looks back, and sure enough there was a graveyard they just passed. Peter also sitting opposite Derek next to this strange boy leans back into his seat looking at Derek with a smile, but rather than mock the strange boy, the boys and girls observe silence passing the few remaining graveyards along the route, even though they saw it as a strange request at the time.

They arrive at the site. Now being much older they're not restricted and are allowed to roam but not on their own.

The six spend most of their time together going down to the beach and exploring the huge forest. That same evening they return to the site. They see the strange boy sitting on the ground poking it with a stick on his own. The six approach him.

"What are you doing" Peter asks,

"Nothing"

"Do you want to play with us" Peter asks.

"Yes" he replies.

He sticks with them for the rest of the week. Callum is his name, a pleasant boy around the same age and quite religious, and though he has strange habits he's not a bother to the rest of the group. In fact, they take a liking to him. That aside this year was to be different and would scar Derek for several years to come. There are certain things that can happen during people's lives, but a seven-year-old witnessing an incident he not only should have been protected from, but one that should have been avoided, would inevitably cause some psychological damage to a young mind. The kids are all taken through the Forrest, leading them down the same path he took on his first visit a few years earlier to the beach. From there they walk along the beach till they come across a rock face. The face itself is about thirty-foot-high with a rock about the size of an old mini at its foot. They're told to climb the rock face. The sheer size of it is scary. Most of the kids including Derek are nervous and tell the staff they do not want to do this. But are told they have no say in the matter. This is his first ever climb on a rock even though he's climbed trees and walls, but never climbed rocks. Without any safety harness or any other kind of safety equipment they start one by one to ascend this thirty-foot monster. Most are frightened and shouting they can't do it. As Derek's turn comes, he begins to get more nervous. His hands are already sweating as he grabs the first ledge with one hand putting his foot on another below. He starts to climb. As he gets a quarter of the way up, he looks down and shouts as others did.

"I can't do it."

He can feel his hands all sweaty causing them at times to slip from their grip. He can also feel his legs turning to jelly. He's never felt this frightened before. A voice from the top shouts

"don't look down, keep looking up"!

He does at first but his brain has other ideas and keeps looking down. As he gets higher the intense of his fear gets worse. From up there everything looks small below. He freezes, he can't go any further. He's only about four or five feet from the top, but this is too much. He's terrified. His legs are shaking like jelly. He just wants to go down. The other kids who made it up and those still waiting at the bottom begin to shout.

"go don't stop, you can do it"!

Just as he's done before he started climbing. The person above him begins to give instructions to him on where to put his hands and feet, even though he's still shouting he can't do it.

Their encouragement is beginning to work. Despite the sweat that forces his hands to slip, he slowly follows the instructions until he finally makes it. He gets to the top and stands up. No sooner doing that he loses all sense of balance and drop to the ground at the top of the rock. His legs are no longer working to the demand of his brain. He has to sit at the top of the rock to get his composure back before meeting up with the rest of the group. He's not the only one who has this fear, others do too. It's down to the last three, as they climb, the oldest girl in the group starts. She like Derek and most of the others before her get nervous only this time she's unable to hold on. As she gets a quarter of the way up, she loses her grip and falls. As she does, she lets out an almighty scream as she freely descends and lands on her back, straight onto the rock at the foot of the rock face. Everyone goes quiet. The only sound that can be heard comes from the waves and the Seagulls. Gasps come from the young witnesses. They don't know if she is ok as there's no movement from her. Even the staff who forced her up freeze, either in shock or just not able to react. It's like everything was happening in slow motion. Suddenly a cry comes from her. The staff member moves towards her. She's clearly in pain but eventually is able to get to her feet. Some of the kids are crying from the shock of what they've just witnessed. With slow steps, and help from the staff, she makes her way up with a limp joining the group via another route. She's covered in bruises but seems ok, but rather than walking straight back to the site, they're taken around the area sightseeing along the lake near what looks like a castle, before heading back. After the incident, no one was interested in the tour, they just wanted to go back to the site still shaking over what they had witnessed.

It's the last full day of the holiday at the site, and two men turn up out of the blue and begin digging a hole in the front lawn of the cottage. By evening they light a fire in the hole and place a wire mesh grate over the fire. Food is being cooked over it. Although at the time it didn't dawn on Derek, but it's his first ever Barbecue. In the three years he attended this holiday, it's the first time this has happened. Some of the other kids thought it was to take their mind off the rock incident. The cottage door is opened up and he's able to take a peek inside. One of the men shows him around. It's empty with just a few bits and pieces scattered around. There's no furniture. The man explains to him that no one can live in it because the roof is unsafe.

"luckily he didn't see me and the the other boys climbing on the roof a couple of days ago then" Derek thought to himself.

The roof looks high from the front of the cottage, but there's a small hill at the back giving easy access to the the roof for the small child size body. Other than the rock climbing incident, everything else was ok on the Holiday. The next day they all return back to the home, nothing more was ever mentioned about the incident on the rocks even though it still shook the kids up. Callum, the strange boy also disappeared after they returned. No one knew where he went or why he was even with them. Perhaps he was one of the kids from the mobile unit, there temporarily whilst waiting for a permanent place. The kids from the main building very rarely meet or interact with the occupants of the mobile unit.

A few days later Alan's uncle turns up at the home. They

know him as Uncle John. Alan and his brothers pack a few things as he's taking them to the beach for the day. They leave, but moments later Alan returns telling Derek to grab his swimming trunks. Alan wants him to join him so his Uncle is given permission to take him. They set off. Uncle John turns out to be a bit of a comedian, joking and laughing along the route. It's tight in the back of the car as it's small, though with all the laughter the trip passes quickly as they reach the sea. Uncle John opens his boot telling the two older boys to take the picnic hamper out. They grab each handle carrying it down to the beach. Uncle John carries the only deck chair which he uses. It's hot and almost lunch time, but everyone's too excited to eat so change into their trunks. They all run down to the sea. The two older boys run straight in splashing water everywhere. Alan, Derek, and Uncle John take their time. Uncle John goes in followed by Alan. Derek takes his time walking in then as the water reaches his ankles he runs back out. He finds it too cold. Alan and Uncle John do their best to talk him in, but he's having none of it and stays put at the waters edge where it feels warmer watching the others jump around in the waves. Tom and Archie, Alan's brothers, come out from the sea and grabs Derek laughing as they pick him up carrying him further out into the sea then drop him in the water. He lets out a scream quickly getting to his feet. He's now knee deep in the water. He feels his knees getting use to it and calls Alan over. Archie and Tom are still standing there laughing as Alan gets to him. Alan is smiling and asks him if he ok. Derek replies

"yes"

Alan whispers into his ear and both start splashing Alan's brothers. Uncle John shouts "you deserved that".

before joining in siding with Alan and Derek. After a while playing, they make their way to the hamper on the beach. Uncle John had already spread the picnic blanket out before going into the sea. Archie turns to Derek saying.

"Derek, sorry we threw you in".

Derek looks at him and the others, saying.

"I've never had as much fun as I did today".

They laugh whilst eating and drinking, but sadly it's the last time they would have such a time together, as a week later the three brothers are to leave. Although Derek had many friends in the home, it was that moment on the beach that had a lasting effect on him. He felt part of Alan's family for those several hours he was with them and all because his best friend chose to make him feel part of it for that moment. On the day they are leaving Derek stands in front of them just outside the office saying goodbye to all three of them as they stand in a line. None of them are smiling. Archie and Tom shake his hand, but as Alan grabs Dereks hand, he lets go stretching his arms around Derek literature hugging him. Derek stands there not sure how to react. No one has ever put their arms around him before. Eventually he responds in the same way. Derek walks with them to the door watching them load uncle Johns car. Then as they get in the car they wave as they leave the driveway leaving the gates. Matron puts her hand on Derek's shoulder guiding him back into the house. It's the last time he sees them. He's not too upset as he still has his other friends joining up with them in the back garden.

Chapter 19
Second Foster

A new school year has started. Derek is still struggling with his schoolwork and seems to be way behind his fellow classmates. He's sent to a specialist where he has to visit for a while every week asking him to do a series of tasks like putting shapes in the correct slots, showing him pictures of animals and objects, and asking him what comes into his head. The only problem he knows he has is being left-handed, not having the best handwriting and juggling with words that seem to have a mind of their own. Other than that he feels normal. He was never told he's dyslexic, that he would find out many years later. But still he's seen as a slow learner and academically insecure.

A few months during that year he's put up for either adoption or foster care for the second time. Still in Glasgow though in an area more open. At first things go well and he's adapting well. His new family have other children though he's not sure if they too are adopted or fostered. He starts at a new School and is enjoying his time with the family and the School which is far more open than his previous two. The land around his school is open giving him some memories of his first Home, though without the sea. School is a modern building of its time. The teacher spends time with him recognising he does have problems and taking the time to give him a one-to-one approach after setting tasks for the rest of the class. She never gets frustrated with him unlike his previous teachers and he now feels more secure about himself. The school yard is big and flows onto a school field surrounded by open space. One day after a heavy down pour the children are out in the School yard. It's still warm as the clouds break and the sun hits the tarmac on the school yard. He notices what to him at the time looked like smoke rising off the ground. It was the rainwater on the ground rising and evaporating, but he didn't know that. He found it strange but exciting. He's never seen this before and wants to know more about it. As the day goes on and the teacher continues with her usual teaching stuff. The only thing on his mind is this strange smoke rising from the ground. Questions are going through his mind wondering what caused it, why did the whole yard go up in smoke and why there was no fire. The School day ends and he walks to the teacher speaking to her about what he saw, she explains about the rain and heat and how it causes water to evaporate and what he was seeing was water particles rising off the ground as steam from the heat of the sun. He was never confident asking his teacher at his last school anything as she never seemed to have time for him or the others in the class. As he goes outside the kids from the house are waiting for him,

"come on" one says as Derek runs towards them.

The other kids treat him as part of the family taking him to the local park and roaming the streets. But he never felt for them how he felt for Alan and his family. His time with his new family sadly doesn't last long. One day something causes him to become aggressive and violent. To this day he doesn't recall what triggered this anger and why he punched the window of a door causing both it to smash and his hand to bleed. But within two days he's back at the home where he left only a month or two earlier. As gutted as he is, he had to accept what he did was wrong, though could never understand why.

He's now back at Eversley and returning to his old school. He's back in the same class he was in when he left and fitting back in quite well. He's back with his friends Alan McKenzie now his best friend and still hanging around with Frank, Jimmy and Peter when he's not with his age group. The rest of that year goes on like any other year with the exception of one strange period.

Sometime before Christmas the home puts on a show. For a few weeks, most of the kids are pushed to rehearse dance routines, songs and sketches. Most of them are not interested, but as they've repeatedly come to expect. They have no say in anything that goes on. Derek along with a dozen others will be doing the fling. After weeks of rehearsals the performance night comes. The stage is at the top end by the door leading to the garden. The mobile unit is used as the changing rooms. It's a cold night and now in a kilt, Derek and his dance team head to the playroom from the outside. The door opens and as they walk-in, the last act walks out passing them. Once in it becomes daunting. The room is full of strangers. People they don't know with the exception of the staff. They're all dressed up in suits and dresses staring at them. The performance starts and as much as everything went perfectly during the rehearsal, their nerves get the better of them and everything falls apart. They can hear the laughter as they feel the humiliation just raring to get out. Finally, with the disastrous performance over, they make their way back to the mobile unit to the annoyance of the staff member responsible for guiding them through the performance. At least they were never punished for it, most likely because the sham performance was probably more entertaining.

Christmas arrives, but this Christmas is not the same like

with every year standing under the clock in the main entrance as all the others leave. But the difference this time is two remain. Derek and one new boy recently arrived about the same age Derek was when he joined. He goes over to the stairs and they both sit on the bottom step tired of standing, sitting at each side of the wide staircase occasionally glancing at each other but don't socialise. Derek is waiting for Moreen to tell him to get ready, but that isn't to be. She's away this Christmas. Matron comes to explain she's on sick this week and wouldn't be able to take him this year. She takes them both into the staff room where they spend most of the morning watching tv still keeping a distance. After dinner, Matron brings board games in and joins them explaining the rules and playing along with them. Both are now interacting and he learns the wee boy's name is Alastair. Sometime later both get bored with the games and Derek asks if he could go outside to play. It's cold but dry. Matron agrees but says.

"I need you both to stay together",

"I'll look after him outside" he says,

Alastair smiles as he hears this.

"Go on then, put your coats and wellingtons on".

she says. Following her instructions both go to the cloakroom. Alastair struggles with his wellies so Derek helps him put them on then with their coats and wellies on, they make their way to the door next to the cloakroom. It's locked. Derek tells Alastair to follow him. He goes looking for Matron eventually finding her. She tells them to use the kitchen door. Out they go. It's cold and windy, but that doesn't stop them both going straight to the swings. Alastair sits on one while Derek sits on the other. Derek notices Alastair sitting but not swinging.

"can't you swing" he asks him,

"no" he replies,

Derek remembers the time he was in this very situation and how Moreen helped him. He does the same to help Alastair. As he gets confident, both are swinging and singing songs they're making up as they go along only to see Matron and another staff member giggling from the staff room window directly in front of them, instantly both going quiet with embarrassment. As the early night draws in, both go back into the house. This year there is no Christmas dinner and both being the only two left sleep in the same room that night. When they wake up the next morning, they're joined by others who returned throughout the night.

Another year gone and now 1973. One month and a week into this new year and Derek celebrates his 8th birthday with his home mates. That same Month February, he starts Cubs at the local Scout group. There's an arrangement between the home and the Scout group to take the kids from the home, both boys a girls as they have brownies in the group as well. He's taken there by other kids from the home, but before leaving he's given a uniform to wear. A green jumper, the same grey shorts he wears to school, grey socks, his black school shoes and a green cap with yellow piping running down around the cap. They walk up to the scout hut on Glencairn Drive right next to Glencairn Church. It's a fair distance to walk during the dark freezing cold nights. And in tight shorts were not a comfortable thing for him during the cold winter nights and the only part of his scouting experience he hated. But for the first time in his life he's found something he really enjoys. The activities are great. Akela is cool, but his assistant is always hitting them on the head with his metal whistle. But unlike some staff members at the home he never singles anyone out, though as painful as it was, It didn't take the enjoyment out of him or the other cubs. Those early days of his time in cubs will shape what he does years into the future, and still sees many of the traditions being acted on to this day, though with a modern twist. He continued his time in Cubs till the day he leaves the home and gets involved in almost everything to do with the group. Coffee mornings, though not keen on the cheek nippers mostly from the old biddies. He enjoyed doing the bob-a-job, visiting locations around Pollockshields, clearing gardens, helping with shopping. There are times particularly with the old people they would give him pennies above what they gave for the cubs to keep for themselves, but chose to add them to the pot.

One of those enjoyable Cub nights were to end painfully when he returned to the home. He with his friends just arrived back and are told to get ready for bed as with most nights when they arrive back. Derek and his friends still hyped up from that evening at cubs are jumping around in their underwear. Jumping from bed to bed till he feels a slap on his behind. He looks back to find Jill had spanked him and is now chasing the other boys. Derek runs out of the room, downstairs and out the main entrance. Not the best thing to do in his underwear on a freezing cold night, though at that point he didn't care. He looks around and sees the first huge green door fully open. He runs back in and hides behind it. Jill has already raised the alarm, and all the staff members are now looking for him. They pass him umpteen times calling his name and not once thinking of looking behind the door. He starts feeling the cold as it gets even later and waits for a chance to find a new hiding place indoors. As soon as the voices go quiet he sees his chance and makes his way back through the second door then into the dining room hiding at first under the tables. He realises he'll easily be seen, so he goes behind the bay window curtains completely blocking his view from the dining room itself as the curtains are full size from above the window to the floor. They don't go into the bay, which means he's completely oblivious to the fact he's now in full view from outside the huge bay windows. Now caught he's taken to the Matrons office and given a useless lecture from her before getting hit on his hand by her ruler then sent to bed.

There's never a dull moment when a group of kids live together in an environment where TV is barely noticed even though it sits above a shelf in the dining room constantly on except for nights. Where computer consoles are not yet invented, and electronic toys are still in their infancy. Where kids just did the most outrageous and craziest things just to kill time. Peter is one of those kids who does anything to draw attention to himself. It's one of the reasons he's the most popular kid in the home. At times he will drag others into his mischievous, and at times inappropriate antics. On this particular Saturday lunch time he's no different. As the weather warms and the rain pours the kids just run around the house. Dinner has only just finished and Derek see's Peter sliding with his back to the floor with his friends laughing as they slide back and forth, "what are you doing" Derek asks,

Peter puts his finger to his mouth to signal him to keep quiet whilst laughing, then signals Derek to join him telling him to copy him. He waits for the dinner lady to gather the empty plates from the table. At that moment sliding out to look up the skirts, then sliding back in to avoid being seen. But Peter being Peter will do anything to amuse himself. Later in the afternoon still as the rain falls Jill takes Derek and a few others from his dorm to his favourite place, the transport museum at the bottom of Albert Drive next to the railway not far from the home. It's all inside and a trip he enjoys though the visits are not as frequent as he would like. Inside they get hands on experience getting on the old busses, trams and engines. Upstairs is the restaurant where they're treated to pop-up and ice cream delicacies before heading back home.

Chapter 20
Fire incident

School has just Broken up for Summer and this will be Derek's last summer at Eversley and the most memorable for all the wrong reasons, one that would haunt him for life knowing he was part of a group of boys involved in an incident that most likely scared one of his friends physically for life.

It's the first week of the Summer holidays and the younger group have already left for the caravan site. Derek is due to go next week. It's hot and he and his friends are bored as the older boys leave to go to the park. They wanted to go, but the older kids preferred to go on their own and not have the need to care for the younger kids. With nothing to do they just hang around the back garden trying to keep themselves occupied as much as they can. One remaining older boy approaches Derek and his friends asking if they want to have fun. He's older than the rest and pretty much a loner. His name is Tom, and he leads Derek, Alan McKenzie, Frank and Jimmy from the home sneaking out the front and walking into a neighbour's front garden. The owners are away on holiday, and it's clear Tom has already been there before. It's a hot summers day and Tom pulls out a box of matches and a can of lighter fuel from his pocket. Where he got them from remains unknown. He's about a year or two older than the others nine or ten. He says.

"let's light a fire".

then tells the others to get wood. The garden they're in is the front garden, and like the home, it too is big though a quarter of the size hidden by bushes and bramble. With the hot summer there is plenty of dead wood to collect, so there is no need to take any live twigs etc, and besides the one thing they don't have is a knife.

As they get the wood and bramble together, the only clearing they have is between the front door and the bramble. They set the pile about 4 metres from the front door. Tom, who has the lighter fluid squeezes the tin allowing the fuel to spray over the pile they've just setup and lights it is causing it to burst into flames. The fire is short lived and as it begins to go out, Tom aims the tin in the direction of the fire squeezing the tin causing it to tilt upwards jetting its contents on to the ankles of Frank who's standing opposite him on the other side of the fire. As he lets go squeezing, the tail end of the fuel catches fire as it falls to the flames causing a stream of flame trialling the fuel at speed onto Frank's ankles catching fire. His ankles are covered by the denim of his jeans giving him some protection from both the flame and heat, but he starts to panic and starts kicking his legs in fear. This causes the fire to flare up more eventually penetrating his jeans. Tom runs to him and pushes him to the ground. Screaming in agony he starts rolling around, it's clear he's in pain. Tom stamps on his legs quickly putting the fire out. The screaming from Frank is piercing as he continues kicking his legs in pain. As well as being worried about Frank, the boys know they're in big trouble, but none of them run away. They know he isn't able to walk himself. Tom and Alan McKenzie take each side of Frank putting his arms over their shoulders taking most of his weight. He stops screaming but he's still crying. As they enter the house from the main entrance, Jill and another staff member are there talking to each other. Jill seeing the damage to him starts to panic,

"What happened".

She says as she starts fuming and shouting at the boys,

"What happened" she asks again.

"He got burnt".

Tom says as Jill and the other staff member take care of Frank. Another staff member emerges from the nursery most likely from hearing the commotion. Jill takes Frank in one direction helped by the first staff member.

"Take them up to the office".

She tells the remaining staff member. The boys are taken to the office and told to wait outside as matron isn't there. It feels like hours standing there nervously with all sorts of things going through their minds not knowing what to expect. They know it's serious and that they will expect to get punished. They also know they will deserve it.

With the exception of Tom, the others feel bad about what happened. Frank is their friend and they're worried about him wishing they could turn the clock back. Their wait is only about 15 minutes then Jill comes back along with Matron taking them into the office. She begins to lecture them, then tells them what punishment would be given to them. First it's the ruler to the hand, it's certainly a few blows on each hand. Next they are told to strip down. They take their clothes off standing only in their underwear. Derek now fears this will be worse than Barbara. He hasn't forgotten what stripping down meant.

"everything" she says,

there's a pause. The boys look at each other,

"NOW" she shouts,

with that, they take their remaining clothes off. She takes them out to the landing and make them sit in four separate areas. They are to spend the next three day sitting in the same place, allowed only to move for breakfast, Lunch, dinner, bed and toilet. They're not allowed to speak to each other though they do when no one's around. Then they're told they will not be going to the caravan. They feel gutted at that as it's the one event they always look forward to.

They sit out in the landing with their knees tucked as tight as possible to hide their private parts. Tom owned up to having the matches and lighter fluid and says it was his idea. By now it's already got around to everyone else about what happened. As Peter comes up stairs, he kicks Tom on the first day as he walks past him swearing at him, angry that he got his friends involve and causing the injury to Frank. Peter is short for his age, but he's tough. Moreen grabs him holding him back as Matron calms him down. On the second day Tom is not with them. His space is empty. The boys find out later in the day he's gone from the home, as too is Frank, though it's likely Frank is in hospital. They ask about Frank, but they're never told about his condition, where he is, or when he'll be back. Derek will never see him again for his remaining time at the home. The boys are bored, now sat in their pyjamas with nothing to do, occasionally talking to each other when no staff members are watching.

On day three they're eventually allowed to move but not leave the house. They're still not given their clothes back, so spend most of their morning in the playroom, mostly looking out of the windows watching their other home mates playing in the rear garden. Watching them running around on the swings, down the right side of the garden near the bottom corner in the sand pit wishing they could be out there with them. Lunch is called, but they're told to remain in the playroom until they're called. With the dining room only several metres from where they are, they can smell the food as well as hear the kids. Now sat on the benches eagerly waiting to be called. Their thoughts are that they are not going to get fed today as part of their punishment is beginning to set in. Jimmy the timidest of the three is beginning to tear up. Both Derek and Alan McKenzie are trying to console him. The dining room goes quiet as the noise moves to the backdoor slamming as the other kids make their way outside again. The boys are making their way back to the window when footsteps are heard coming towards the door. They quickly sit down again as the door opens. It's Jill,

"go on, go to the dining room" she tells them,

As they walk in, everything is already set out though cold as it's been since the punishment began. But at least they were being fed. After Lunch they're sent back to the playroom again staring out the window till it got to a point where Derek decides he's had enough. It may have been that day or the day after, but everyone else is outside playing whilst they are stuck inside.

"I'm going outside" Derek tells his two mates,

"you'll get into more trouble" Alan McKenzie tells him,

"I don't care" he replies.

He spends no time planning his escape route, he strips off to the shock of his friends,

"What are you doing" Alan McKenzie asks,

Jimmy just stares saying nothing, and Derek just smiles at both leaving the playroom in his birthday suite, most likely a dare on his part or from one of his friends as he was often a sucker to dares, passing the door that leads to the rear garden, through the dining hall, across the main entrance hall, down the corridor and past the kitchen, then outside via the kitchen side door to avoid the staff member standing between the door that leads directly outside from the playroom, and the door from next to the dining room, knowing she was only there to stop them going out. He's running around until he hears Matron's voice shout his name pretending not to hear her. The other kids point to the kitchen side door where her voice is coming from, he sees a couple of staff members running towards him. He has no choice but to look.

"GET OVER HERE NOW"

shouts the voice again, this time he begins to walk over. His head is full of "what will happen now?" will it be the ruler again? Will I have to sit on the landing again? As he gets closer, Matron says.

"what do you think you're doing, get inside".

her tone is angry but she's not fuming. He's taken up to his bedroom where his other two accomplices are waiting. They're given their clothes back and warned never to do anything like that again. They quickly put their cloths on and join the rest outside. From that point onwards, it became obvious to Derek, he's looked at as a troublemaker.

Holidays will be over soon, but still, it's hot and the staff decide to take the paddling pool out. Excited the kids are getting ready to jump in, but they're told to go and play till they're called over. As soon as the pool is filled with water, it becomes obvious why. The staff decide to use it to have fun themselves, throwing each into the pool leaving the kids just watching and waiting for their turn. The kids are laughing to begin with, but as time goes on, the staff continue to play amongst themselves. When they're finally finished, the kids start running over to get their chance to jump in and cool off only to be told.

"it's getting late, you'll get your chance another day".

That other day never materialises.

Summer ends, and as Autumn sets in, the mobile unit that's sat in the garden long before Derek arrived at the home, and used mostly for temporary residents waiting permanent residency either at Eversley or other homes is being towed away. It was not the easiest of tasks for them to get it out from the garden as Derek and others cheer and laugh as they watch the live comedy show from the dining room bay window, as the driver attempts to get the huge object on to the road. With staff trying to guide him with some almost disastrous results, almost taking the concrete gate post out with him.

Chapter 21
Too Young to Shave

It's Christmas Eve and everyone in bed is usually sound asleep, but not Derek, he struggles at times to sleep. This is something that will stick with him right though his adult years too. Sometime during the middle of the night, one of the staff member's is placing chocolate stockings on the foot of each bed. It's difficult to see who it is as the only light source is coming from the landing with the door open. The staff member is startled by Dereks voice.

"You're not Santa". Derek says

The staff member looks over. Derek is looking straight at her stopping her in her tracks.

"You should be asleep".

She says as she starts collecting the stockings again, then leaving the room. Eventually Derek does falls asleep waking up on Christmas Day to find the stockings back on all the beds. Then as with every Christmas it's the tradition of standing under the huge clock in the main entrance hall hoping a relative would come and take him, wishful thinking on his part, as he's come to terms that he's all alone with no relatives. He also expects to be held back with Alastair again, who is for the second year is with him along with another boy, John, similar in age to Alastair. This time all three are sitting on the bottom step though this time they're socialising more than they did last year as Alastair already knows the other boy, and Derek and Alastair are now friends even though they never play together, it's more symbolic. This time Moreen appears given all three a smile, as she looks after those two.

"Come on" she says,

as Derek stands up walking towards her.

"You're going to have company this time".

she says as she points to the other two signalling them to come over. The two other boys are going to be joining him this year. Moreen takes them telling Derek it will only be for the day as she could not take all three to her home, disappointed as it's almost a repeat of the last time, but Derek understood this. Again, as like two years ago, she takes them to her parent's flat in a high-rise block, and like that time, Moreen had already made plans before their arrival and all three will have their Christmas dinner there, though in true child investigatory opportunity, nothing ever goes as smoothly as adults hope. After dinner, Derek goes to the toilet. There on the sink is a razor with shaving soap right next to it. It's tempting as he washes his hands with his eyes fixated on the shaving tool throughout. Hands washed he starts to dry them with his eyes still fixated on this device. After he dries them, he puts his hand on the door handle and then looks back at the sink where these objects sit temptingly and invitingly to his ever-exploratory eyes. He walks over to the sink again staring at the shaving tools looking towards the door as if someone was going to walk in, then it happens. He touches the handle of the razor getting a good feel of it while continually looking towards the door hoping no-one walks in even though it's locked from his side. He then lifts the razor out from the jar that holds it blade up. A shaving mirror sits on the other side of the sink. After another glance at the door, that too is lifted with his other hand. He looks into the mirror, then looks at the blade of the razor constantly looking over to the door every few seconds or so out of nervousness. He takes the blade side of the razor to his chin, and with a single pull, he feels the end of the world falling in on his head. Blood is dripping from his chin. He drops the blade and puts his finger over the cut. Moreen's voice comes from the other side of the door.

"Are you ok, you're taking a long time, john needs to go in".

"I'ye, I won't be long".

He says, now panicking knowing full well he's in a lot of trouble.

"Well don't be long" says Moreen,

"ok" he replies.

He feels no pain, though that maybe some consolation of what's to come. The blood just isn't going to stop. He tries to wash it with water, wiping the blood, but that only makes matters worse as it's smudges across his face. Now realising he has to take his chance, he slowly unlocks the door, puts his hand on the handle and slowly opens it. John is standing on the other side He takes one look at his now blood-soaked face and runs into the lounge screaming.

"Derek has blood all over him".

no sooner from that, Moreen runs through, sees him and says.

"what happened",

"nothing" he replied,

"why is your face covered in blood",

"i don't know".

he says, as the voice of her mum shouts

"is everything ok Moreen".

Moreen doesn't reply. She drags him into the bathroom as John stands by the toilet having a wee whilst staring at the damage to Derek's face. Moreen washes his face in cold water for what feels like hours, eventually stopping the blood. As they leave the toilet the floor is covered in blood, almost like a murder scene. They make their way into the lounge where a plaster is placed over the wound and then it happens. She goes into Judge, Jury and executioner role,

"were you using the razor", she asks,

and like every criminal, Derek goes into denial mode,

"no" he replies with a short pause before adding.

"I never touched it",

"then why is it covered in blood" she asks,

"I don't know".

is the only reply he could come up with. She looks at him, and says,

"I'm very disappointed in you. What you did was wrong, but then to lie only makes it worse, and you have to be punished for that".

today will be the one and only time Derek is to feel real pain from her hand. He could see in her face how upset she is, more because they both knew deep down, she had to do it. With everyone watching, she sits on the dining table chair and instructs him to get over her knee. No sooner over, the blows rained down. It isn't excessive like what Barbara did, but hard enough to bring tears. And unlike Barbara, she never took his trousers down. Shortly after that, they leave the flat, and returned to the home.

Another year has gone and now into 1974, life goes on as normal. Derek finally gets his chance to go with his friends and some of the older boys to the local park. It's freezing cold, but still, they go as a group making their way to Maxwell Park, not far from the home, roughly the same distance as it is to the Scout hut. Once there they walk through the park to the far end where the pond is. This is Dereks first time there. He usually goes to Queen's Park with the staff but its much further and much bigger. The pond is frozen. Ice has formed on the the surface, with other local kids sliding on it. As they approach, the boys joining them mostly seem to know each other. One of the boys from the home thought it smart to jump on the ice. Bad move. As he does his legs go straight through the ice into the pond. It's only up to just above his knees, but the shock from the freezing water causes him to fall with his chest in the water. A few others go over to help him but with the ice already broken, they too end up in the water to the amusement of all around some laughing hysterically. Eventually they're out, but now have to figure how to get back without being caught. They decide just to hang around, play football and run around to try and keep warm as well as dry out. The other two are not too bad, they mostly got soaked from the thighs down. The boy who went chest down was struggling at first, for a good 30 minutes or so. His friend gives him his coat, but he's still shivering. After a while one of the boys tells him to take his tops off. He does, removing his jumper, shirt and vest, then wraps himself in the coat eventually giving him some comfort. At some point they have to return. His tops are still soaked, so he can't wear them. Two boys his size take one layer of tops off themselves handing it to him. He discards his own tops as that would have been a giveaway. By now their trousers are damp as they return back to the home. No one noticed so they got away with it.

Chapter 22
Redhouse

Not much happened until after his 9th Birthday in February. Most kids leave this home around the age of twelve to fourteen and there's already talk of Derek leaving soon, but no time given. Then later in February his social worker Mr Black turns up out of the blue, particularly more so as he had no idea he had a social worker, or what one even is. On top of that, he also had no idea Mr Black was his social worker from the day he was left at Brairvadach near Rue at the age of 7 weeks.

Matron calls Derek as she stands next to Mr Black. She introduces Derek to him telling him he would like to talk with him. They go upstairs, then she points to a room where they both go into as she walks off. He takes him in leaving the door open and sits him and himself on one of the beds in the room. It's one of the smaller bedrooms. Mr Black tries to explain who he is and what a social worker is, but he just looks at him as if he some kind of alien barely listening to a word he's saying, though his attention is suddenly caught when he starts asking him what he thought about moving to a new Home. Derek was already made aware he would be moving soon but didn't expect it to come from a complete stranger. He gives him a choice, another home in Glasgow or a Home near the seaside. He told him about both homes saying the home in Glasgow is Downcraig, another mixed home a short distance from Eversley, or Red House, an all-boys home near the sea. Derek thought for a moment as he's made many friends here and thoughts were going through his head that he may never see them again. He's distracted for a while as he looks around the room. It's the first time he's been in this room as it's the girls bedroom. But he knows the surroundings, the moulded ceilings, the panelled doors, the door handle, the beds, all of them are familiar items he took for granted until that moment as they are throughout the house. Now his thoughts had to be focused on the future. He still remembers the views of the sea from Blairvadach and that was to sway his decision. After a while he chooses Red House.

"You'll like it there" he said,

"when will I be going" he asked,

"it'll be a couple of weeks",

with that, he stands up and leaves saying.

"I'll be in touch".

Derek sits there for a while trying to digest what had just happened as it sinks in. A few minutes later, Matron stands by the door asking him if he is ok.

"yes" he replies,

"I hear you chose the seaside" she says,

"yes" he replies,

"go on, join your friends" she says.

With that he leaves the room.

For days he has mixed feelings about leaving. His friends

become aware he's leaving but as the weeks come and go he hears nothing. Maybe it was all just a dream he thought. Then Matron tells him he would be going in a few days. He feels down. A lot has happened here, and he's about to lose his friends the one thing he's not looking forward to. One or two days before he leaves, he plays in the sandpit alone at the bottom of the garden. His back is to the house, and its still winter and cold, but dry and sunny. He hears a voice saying,

"can we play".

he looks around. It's Alastair and John with Moreen standing at a distance in the background looking on,

"if you want" he says,

they join him, then Alastair says,

"Moreen said you're leaving".

he looks around, she's still standing a distance away looking. He looks back at Alastair and says.

"yes, I am",

"we had fun" Alastair said,

Derek smiles without answering,

"remember how you taught me to swing".

Alastair says pointing to the swings,

"yes"

"and we sang that silly song".

"yes", he replies with a smile,

Alastair and John both smile and stand up.

"We'll miss you at Christmas".

Alastair says as they both start walking away towards Moreen saying.

"Goodbye"

Derek looks at them as they walk away, then replies with the same word.

That's the last time he would see them both.

A few days later the moving day comes. It's March 27th, and a week or two before Easter, he's packed and ready to make the move. He leaves by taxi accompanied to his delight by Moreen heading to the train station. They both get on the train starting their journey to Edinburgh. As they travel, they talk, though Moreen is doing most of the talking. He can see she's upset. About halfway through the journey she hands him a bag and says

"keep this for Easter".

He looks inside the bag and sees it's a chocolate Easter

egg. She then reaches over and takes both Derek's hands as they sit opposite each other separated by a table where their hands rest,

"I need to tell you something" she says,

but she sits there saying nothing for a while just holding both his hands with her thumbs doing circular motions on the palm of his hands and staring at him. Then she says,

"this is difficult but you need to know".

she pauses again, but as Derek looks into her eyes, he could see her eyes going red as they water up, but no tears are running.

"I tried to adopt you".

She says pausing as Derek looks bewildered,

"do you understand that" she asks.

He nods his head sideways to say no. Even though he has been adopted or fostered, it's the first time he's heard the word been said. She explains to him what it means in a way he's able to understand, then goes on to say,

"I wanted to adopt you, but because I'm living alone and working, they felt I would not be able to care for you".

Derek listens, but says nothing. She carries on talking, but deep down he wished she did adopt him. He always felt safe around her as she was able to give him what no other person in his nine years could. Love, though vague in its meaning to him, it's what he observed from seeing other families. And to him, his time with Moreen is the closest he felt he ever came to having a mother.

The train is pulling into Edinburgh station and Moreen tells him to grab his bag. She grabs his case then they both get off the train. They take a bus to the historic town of Musselburgh. His eyes are fixated on the sea that could be seen between the houses down the side roads as the bus nears Musselburgh eventually coming in sight of the harbour. He quickly glances at the boats until the harbour becomes obscured by the shops. As they go along the road now out of sight of the sea, they cross a bridge with a flowing river beneath it, the bus stops shortly after. They make their way on foot from the bus stop walking down a one-way street and finally coming in sight of Red House Home where he will spend his last years in a Children's home. They get to the gate where Derek stops for a moment to gaze at what looks like an 18th century Victorian mansion which backs on to the river Esk. The same river he crossed moments ago by bus, and about 200 metres from the mouth to the river forth. The garden is already in full spring with a colourful array of flowers in full bloom as they make their way down the path to the front door. Moreen rings the bell. They look at each other both nervously as the noise of the old-style handle turns from the inside. A chubby lady opens the door and politely asks them to enter introducing herself as Mrs Duncan, though anyone who knew Mrs Duncan knew she was anything but polite. They enter and both ladies start chatting. Derek's mind is elsewhere looking around.

The hall is nowhere near as big as both his previous homes. The door to the right as you enter is the office.

The door to the left the tv room. Ahead there's a split. On the left is the stairs that lead to the private living area and the Attic. The boys are not allowed to use these first flight of stairs until after the first floor. To the right of the stairs is a passage that leads to the staff room (to be), and the main corridor.

After the introductions they're given a tour. They enter the office. Ahead is the desk. To the left of that is a door that leads to the play hall though you have to go through two sets of doors to get there. The play hall is big with three high windows on one end, and four windows along the side with plenty of light coming through them. They have steel mesh protectors on the outside, most likely to protect the windows from the football being played in the yard. They walk over to the door that the boys use which leads onto the main corridor which is "L" shaped. They turn right which takes them to the wash area and back door. As they get to the end, to their left are the sinks, showers and bathroom. The sinks are all in a line back-to-back, with ten on each row set along the middle of the room. On the walls are hooks all numbered with wash bags hanging from them. Derek is taken to the far end.

"That's your bag".

Mrs Duncan tells him as she points to the bag on the hook that has the number 10 on,

"and that's your number" she adds.

From that point onwards, every clothing item including socks, underwear and school wear bore the number 10 on the tags and sewn into items like the socks. There are skylights dotted all over the ceiling. They walk over to the shower room. It's open with no doors. Inside there's six shower heads. A member of staff would always stand by the entrance whilst the boys shower making sure they made three turns in the first cold shower on our way out.

The next room is the bathroom, that does have a door with two cast iron bathtubs. They exit that part and turn left through the laundry area which doubles up as the cloakroom. At the end, and to the right are the toilets which houses around 6 cubicles and a urinal. As they come out from the cloak room to their left is the back door which is the only door the boys are allowed to use and leads out to the yard. To their left are a row of sheds with two garages. One for the Duncan's own car, and the larger one for the caravanette with a larger open shed on the end most likely the original stables. Ahead is the sand pit and Mr Duncan's workshop. As well as running the home he's also a carpenter, and a good one too. To their right is the fire escape that is connected to all the floors apart from the rooms above the dining hall. The boys would often climb onto the roofs via the fire escape that leads to the flat roof above the toilet block, then a short jump that takes them onto the sheds and garage. They're never told not to. As they walk back in, they turn left back onto the main corridor. The door to their left is the cleaning cupboard and as they go back to where the play hall door is, they turn right to the longest part of the corridor. They walk up and to their left is the window to the staff room (to be), followed by the narrower corridor that leads to its door and the main front entrance. They then continue as they come across two doors on either side. The door to their left leads to the tv room and the door to their right leads to the kitchen. As they enter the kitchen, there's units along the left going into an L shape layout. In the middle of the kitchen is a huge table, to the right a huge range cooker, and as they walk through to the back area are two huge steel drums of milk, a large fridge, and sinks. Further round the back is the sewing room. To their left the pantry and room where the boys have to do the washing up as part of their chores. As they go beyond that, a door leads to the back stairs and a garden which is well maintained.

Leading back in they come to the back stairs that are the only stairs they're allowed to use to get to the first floor, but before going up, they go through the door back onto the main corridor and in front of them is a half closed/half glass wall that leads into the dining hall. It's big. The tables are square and sit four going up one side of the hall along the top then back down along the other wall. On the left wall is a small window that joins with the tv room and a door further up leading into that same tv room which is closed off. They're in the extended part of the building and like the Play hall the windows are high allowing plenty of light to enter. On the wall directly opposite the door, there's a rota for the washing up.

They turn back out through the dining hall door then left through the door that leads to the stairs which are wider than the stairs by the main entrance. Up they go passing a huge window that's arched at the top turning right at the platform and right again to reach the top. There are two toilets to their right and just on queue as Derek by now is desperate for a number two, thus proceeding to leave his mark for the first time at his new dwelling. He can hear them mumbling as he's sitting in the cubicle. After finishing they proceeded with the tour. Opposite the toilets is a door that leads to a staff bedroom. They turn right to a small narrow L shaped corridor that leads to two bedrooms. On the right the first one holds six beds and visible by a window that covers the length of the wall. At the far end bed is a large David Bowie poster. The room after that has three beds, then at the end of the corridor, theres a door that leads into another bedroom that has a few steps to walk down. It has eight beds. The first bed on the right has a poster of Bruce Lee from Enter the Dragon above it, he only died a year earlier. To the far left is a window that opens up like a small door and leads to the fire escape.

They walk ahead through the room that leads to another door that opens up into the first floor of the front entrance stairwell. Its dark with no windows to allow day light to enter. They lead up to the attic as well as the Duncans residence. Up they go. The stairs are narrow and the rail is dark perhaps oak part worn from years of usage. The small platform before the attic leads to the toilets on the right. The final flight leads them to the attic where there are two doors on both left and right. The door to the right is the bigger of the two rooms set with five beds on the left, and four on the right.

They finally go into the last room. On the right side are three beds with three more on the left with the fire escape in between the first two beds.

"That's your bed".

says Mrs Duncan pointing to the bed on the far left with the floor covered in brown altro.

"You can unpack and put your things in the cupboard over there".

pointing to the cupboard on the end nearest to the window.

"We'll go down and get things sorted, then I'll come and see you later".

Moreen looks over to him. Derek can see tears in her eyes. It's the first time he's seen an adult cry. He looks away unable to comprehend or react not knowing what to do. She goes over to him and puts her arms around him giving him a hug. He does the same. He's finally got the hug he longed for since the Christmas decoration incident a few years ago when he was too shy to hug then for protecting him, but it also dawns on him that he may never see her again. This may have been the first time he felt emotional and shed a few tears himself. He puts his arms around her again before she leaves making the most of it while he has the chance. It's the first time he's ever hugged an adult. The last and only hug was from Alan, a boy at Eversley who's the same age as him. They were best friends at the time, and it was the day he left with his two older brothers. For Moreen it turns out it was to be the last time they would ever see each other.

So, this is it. He's at his new home. His last home. He unpacks then sits on the bed waiting for Mrs Duncan to return. He waits, and waits, but she doesn't return, so he looks out the window next to his bed and can see the river Esk. He's high enough to see the two bridges side by side further down towards the mouth. He looks across the river to the sight of boys in red blazers walking out from the private school Lorreto's. The leaves on the trees still young from the coming Summer only a month away,

"I like this place" he thinks to himself.

The smell is different from Eversley, it's fresher. Even the air is fresher unlike the fuel guzzling lorries and busses that constantly polluted the air around Eversley. The noisy seagulls fly around as he notices the swans coming from the left side partially blocked by the extended part of the building above the dining room. But still, no-one comes. He sits on his bed again waiting then hears the door opening behind him as the boys start returning back from school.

"alright"

Says a half-broken voice from a tanned skinned tall lanky older teenager. It's the first time he's heard such a sound.

"yes" Derek replies,

"what's your name" the half man asks,

"Derek" he replies,

after he changes from his School uniform into his play clothes and about to leave the room, he asks him why he's sitting on the bed.

"that woman told me she'll come back for me" he said,

"Mrs D" he replied,

"I think so" he replied,

"she'll no be coming back; I'll take you down" he said.

Derek gets up and follows him downstairs,

"my name's Robert"

he said as they walked down following the same route he came up but in reverse. He takes him outside where some of the other boys are already playing. Some kicking a ball around and one by the far wall in the sandpit playing on his own. Robert joins the others playing football leaving Derek watching. Robert is the younger of two brothers but taller. His older brother Tom Reid would leave and join the army later that year. Robert known as Rab to his friends is mischievous, but funny. Derek walks over to the sandpit where the lonely boy plays with his matchbox cars. He looks up at Derek acknowledging his presence and continues to play,

"can I play" Derek asks,

the boy looks at him shrugs his shoulders and says.

"if you want".

Derek sits near him on the small two layered brick wall separating the sandpit from the tarmac yard.

"Are you new" the boy asks,

"yes" he replies,

he gives him one of his collection of cars, and both play making roads in the sand. They never thought of introducing themselves to each other as they're more interested in playing. The boy's name is Brian, short for his age but same height as Derek with learning difficulties. Over time you learn how to deal with Brian and know when to back off. He's never aggressive, but does have mood swings at any given time, and the sign would be his tongue curling in on itself. When you see this, you know to step away. More often he prefers to keep himself to himself but would help if asked. Often Derek would play cars with him either in the sandpit or in most cases, in the Play hall on a table in the far corner behind the office door.

As time goes on more boys join in playing football . Shortly after a man joins them holding a bunch of keys in his hand jingling around as he runs kicking the ball. Derek asks Brian who he is.

"that's Mr D, he's in charge of the home" he tells him,

"I thought it was that woman" Derek replies.

"No, she's his wife, she thinks she's in charge".

he added. "D" is short for Duncan.

Mr D is good with the boys. His wife Mrs D was pretty much seen as evil, and she truly is. She would nit-pick at every little thing to an extent, Mr D drew a balance between her rule and the boys having fun. If he wasn't there, it would be hell on earth. Mrs D comes outside to call everyone in for tea. As they file in, she clocks on to Derek,

"ahh Mr Nasda, I forgot about you".

she says as he walks past her. No apology, though for his

remaining time in the Home, she never once gets his last name right. They make their way to the dining room. As soon as everyone is sat down the food is brought in by a trolley. Plates and cutlery are already set out just like his previous home except a little more colourful. There's not much conversation going on and most are quiet as they eat. There's another man helping, Mr Dingwall is his name, but some know him as Beardy bob, or Dingy. After dinner the boys are back outside, some stay in the play hall as the cool evening falls in.

It's his first night and bed is 8pm whilst the older boys stay up till 9pm. He's changed and ready for bed. The bed unlike those in the other two homes are normal standard single beds and low. He lies in his bed watching the light rays from the Newhaven lighthouse circling the room almost hypnotising him to sleep. Wakeup call is eight in the morning as the boys getup and change for school before going down to wash before breakfast. As breakfast finishes Derek is left on his own and escorted to the TV room to watch TV. By noon he's bored. The primary school boys come home for dinner. After they leave, Derek decides to explore the home. There's not as many restrictions for roaming around the home as his previous home, so he's able to spend time in his room. Whilst sitting there he notices his Easter egg has disappeared. He looks around for it but it's gone. His first thoughts are someone in the room ate it or hid it. As each of his roommates return from school he asks them about it. They all deny seeing it though one or two are surprised he had one. With no one admitting to having it he decides to ask Mrs D. She tells him she took it for safe keeping and he would get it on Easter Sunday which is only a week or two away. True to her word she gave it to him. After the evening dinner it's time to do the washing up. With the four listed to wash the dishes, they get stuck in. There's three parts to the washing up process. The washing itself followed by the sterilising where everything is put into steel mesh racks and dipped into just hot water, before drying and storing. It's a process that doesn't take long with the boys working together. But it's not just the washing up that's done on a rota. Everything has a specific time. The day you have a bath. The day you have a shower. The day you iron your school uniform. Derek's bath day is Thursdays which is ironic, given shower day is the day after on Friday, leaving him five days to build up plenty of muck.

After the Easter holidays he starts his new school. Musselburgh Burgh Primary school is where he'll spend the next few years until he leaves. His first day goes well pretty much ignored by his classmates, but nothing unusual about a new person on their first day. After School, he walks home with a few others from the home cutting through the derelict land that now sites Eskgreen. A shortcut the boys use till construction takes hold. Ironically that site was originally the old Burgh Primary School demolished a few years before Derek arrives. Now back home, their first task is changing into plain clothes then outside to play. He joins in the football game even though he knows himself he can't play, but just needs to be a part of the gang in his early days at the home. Derek can't help but notice one of the older boys standing by the bike shed staring at him. He's not playing and doesn't talk much, but just keeping himself to himself. Derek just brushes it off as someone looking for attention. At night-time, the younger boys are sent to bed as usual at 8pm, the older boys are sent an hour later, but with Robert in the same room there's never a dull moment and you'll never be expected to sleep early. He's always entertaining keeping the others including the younger boys giggling and laughing to the annoyance of Mrs D who would enter the room telling them off. Then you have the boys from the next room playing with the fire escape hatch set behind both room doors popping their heads in and out. For the boys it's all fun, but for the staff frustration.

Chapter 23
A Close encounter

Another school day and Derek is finally starting to make friends. Some of his classmates like the boys at the home are mischievous, but then that's typical of any school. It's still early days as Derek still gets use to those in his class, and although he stands out from the rest of his class as mixed race, he's never taunted or bullied for it but seemingly accepted by his classmates. It's a school he eventually loves despite his disabilities in terms of academics. His first few months at this school before the summer break are quite memorable in many ways. Bringing cardboard boxes and using them as part of a class project to build a huge robot. It's the kind of project he enjoys as it gets him out of reading and writing and one he would use as part of a project with his Cub scouts many years later in pretty much the same way. Another time again as part of a school project when they have to choose a subject to relay in front of the whole class, and despite not doing much research if any on his chosen subject of Elephants, he's able to pull it off mainly by guessing the answers to the questions asked by his classmates. The only thing he did know about elephants, is the difference between an African and Indian Elephant only because of the ears even though the teacher clearly was putting him to test asking him,

"How old do Elephants live to".

Derek has absolutely no idea, but knows the average age of humans is seventy thus assumed all living creatures live to the same age.

"About seventy" he replies.

"That's right, well done" she says.

Derek smiling completely relieved his guess was right. He gets home this time armed with homework and as he completes his routine of changing, playing outside then having tea. Mrs D tells him to do his homework in the dining room. He gets his satchel and takes it into the dining room where she's waiting for him. She's already pulled a chair to the sideboard for him then helps him get his books out leaving him alone to do his homework. Shortly after Joe walks in, the boy who kept staring at him days earlier,

"I've come to help you with your homework".

he says as he grabs a chair and pulls it up next to him. He sits there for a while but does little helping. Derek can see him just staring at him like he did outside. He suddenly puts his hand on Derek's knee sliding it up and down. Derek is feeling uncomfortable with this and pushes his hand off. A moment later he tells him.

"I need you to do something for me".

Derek looks at him wondering what. Then without warning he pulls his zip down. Derek is confused wondering what he's up to until he pulls his penis out. Derek becomes nervous, his escape route is blocked by Joe sitting between him and the door. Derek has never experienced this before but he knows it's not right. He stands up.

"I need to go to the toilet".

The only words he can think of at that time as he still tries to figure out a way of getting out of the room. Joe stands up and as he's pulling his zip up Derek makes a break running to the door,

"I need to go to the toilet" repeating himself nervously.

he's scared. He walks down the long corridor looking back to see if Joe's following him. He is, so Derek walks faster and sees him doing the same. As soon as he turns the corner at the end of the corridor, he runs to the toilets and locks himself inside the cubicle. It's a while before Joe goes into the toilets most likely because he's looking in other places first. Derek hears him pacing up and down in the toilets before he stops at the cubicle door.

"I know you're in there" he says,

Derek doesn't say a word,

"I wasn't going to do anything" he says,

Derek still remains quiet. His heart is beating like crazy through fear.

"you better not say anything or I'll kick your head in, and I mean it" he says,

Those words are to haunt Derek for the next two years. Joe stays there for a while trying to force the cubicle door open then stops. Derek hears his footsteps leave the room but remains in the cubicle fearing he might still be there waiting for him to come out. He only comes out when he hears a group of footsteps and voices walk into the toilets.

He leaves with them sticking close behind to them till he feels safe. He needs to get his books but fears getting them in case Joe is there waiting for him. The group he's following turns into the TV room. He stands by the door hesitant looking at the dining room door at the top of the corridor where his books are still scared to go thinking Joe maybe waiting for him. He walks into the TV room and there sitting on the end chair is Joe. Derek wants to tell someone but is fearful of what Joe will do. Joe looks at him with piercing eyes as if to remind him to say nothing. Derek walks out of the room realising he's got his chance now to get his books, quickly running and grabbing them but doesn't go back into the TV room. He doesn't want to face Joe again and goes upstairs to his room finishing his homework still listening out for any footsteps coming up the stairs. As much as he wanted to tell, he feared what might happen, so kept quiet.

The weather warms as the summer months begin. On an evening in the TV room the table is crowded with all the boys trying to glimpse the holiday brochures laid on the table. Derek manages to push himself in.

"what is it" he asks,

"Butlins brochures"

the voice next to him says. It's Derek Haggerty, Haggis for short, smiling with his dimple cheeks, with excitement,

"that's where we're going" he tells him,

Derek's never heard of the place, so doesn't take much notice. Yes, he likes his holidays away. But being so use to caravans and his only interpretation of a holiday, didn't excite him as much, and he tends not to read much because he struggles with seeing the words, so avoids all forms of literature when he can.

"You'll love it" Haggis tells him,

He goes on to explain to him what Butlins is, showing him the photos in the brochure. He's obviously been there before so has in idea of what Derek can expect as this will be His first time going. Haggis has sold it to him. He's now looking forward to it, yet it's still April, so he still has two months of waiting.

Chapter 24
Musselburgh Harbour

The weekend arrives, and the weekly tradition of queuing up outside the office after lunch for their weekly pocket money begins. For Derek he's on the lower pay scale of 50p per week while the older boys get the higher pay grade of a £1 note. With that there's a dash to the local shops shared with the redcoats from the nearby private school Loretto's insight of the historical Old Town Hall, origins of which come from the old Toll Booth. After buying his weekly stash of sugary delights, it's time to explore his surroundings. He was never allowed to go on his own at his previous home, but here he has far more freedom to roam around with some restrictions which are regularly ignored.

Musselburgh is on a much smaller scale than Glasgow and far more open. His eyes caught the harbour the day he moved to Redhouse, but the only areas he's been till today is his route to his school. He walks back through the arch carved into the Musselburgh Arms Hotel leading onto Kerr's Wynd, but instead of turning left onto Millhill that takes him back to Redhouse, he turns right following the road round taking him to the bridges. Now close up to the two bridges he saw from his bedroom window on his first day, he realises the wider bridge is closed and sealed with a gate across it on both ends. The second a much narrower foot bridge mostly of steel construction which looks like a miniature version of a Victorian railway bridge is open. He walks across it as the flow of water from the river Esk widens beneath the bridge as it's so close to the mouth meeting up with the river forth. Not that the fourth is noticeable as a wide river, unless the day is clear of mist. As soon as he's on the other side of the bridge, he follows the Esk towards the mouth taking him to the promenade that runs through Fisherrow park leading him directly to the harbour. As he walks the harbour walls he's taken by the size of the trawlers though few in numbers. He climbs on to the ledge of the harbour wall's end sitting on top of the wall taking in the sights. Fishing nets hung to dry, small sailing and rowing boats moored inside the walls, fishing boats being tended to for maintenance and floors being scrubbed. The smell of dead fish lingers the air as the seagulls circle the harbour waiting for a chance to steal a catch. It's his first intake of the scenery in front of him. The shoreline on both sides with breathtaking views. To his right a huge hill protruding from the relatively flat landscape named Arthur's seat sitting on a redundant volcano and overwhelming the skyline. To his left, Cockenzie power station who's smoking twin towers fill the distant sky, with him slap bang in the middle sitting on the historical landmark of Musselburgh's centuries old harbour in Fisherrow that meets the border of Edinburgh. It's not taken him long to fall in love with this place. As he continues to sit taking it all in, he hears a voice from behind him saying.

"you shouldn't be up there laddie".

Derek turns to look. It's one of the Fishermen in his late twenties or early thirties from one of the trawlers in his yellow waterproof trousers held up with braces,

"it's a big drop on the other side" he continues to say.

Derek looks down to the other side as the waves form to thrash the sandy beach further up. It's high, but the wall is wide.

"come on laddie, I'll gee you a hand dune"

he says as he stretches his hands towards him. Derek moves towards him where he grabs him gently bringing him back to the cobblestone walkway of the harbour walls. He isn't angry or telling him off, but talks to him with respect.

"what were you doing up there" he asks,

"just looking around".

"where's your parent" he asks,

"I don't know" he replies,

"so, who are you with" he asks,

"No-one"

"Where have you come from" he asks.

"I'm from the home" Derek replies,

"ahh Red House" he asks,

"aye" Derek replies,

"Should you be here" the fisherman asks,

"we're allowed out".

"ok, well keep off the wall, it's no safe".

he says as Derek makes his way back.

Now back at the home Derek spends his time outside looking for Brian but he's nowhere to be seen, so he finds a couple of wooden pegs removing the spring from them improvising to make cars using the same patch Brian used on his first day scraping out a road in the sand. It's not thick with sand and has a concrete base. There he spends his time till teatime. As he walks into the call for tea, he bumps into Brian as he's coming out from the play hall.

"I was looking for you Brian" Derek tells him,

"I was playing inside, it's a bit cold outside" he replied,

Though the sun is out, there is a slight chill in the air.

"why were you looking for me" Brian asks,

"I wanted to play with your cars" Derek replies,

"after tea in there"

he says pointing to the Play Hall looking at Derek over the top frame of his glasses while both are making their way to the dining room at the end of the hall. Derek suddenly slows down.

"Brian wait" he says,

Brian looks back and asks "why".

"Just walk with me please",

"ok" he replies,

the reason he slowed down is so as not to bump into Joe who's walking just ahead of him. After tea as agreed, Brian lets him play with his cars.

The next day the boys are up having breakfast then preparing to go to church. With their Sunday best on, they're all bunched together led by the Duncan's as they embark on foot from the home to the Kirk (Church). The first part of the journey follows the same route he takes to school bypassing his shortcut through the derelict land most likely so Mrs D doesn't have to walk over the rubble. Once up the pathway from High street, they turn away from the school on Mansfield road, to Dalrymple Loan, walking up then past the playhouse which is the local cinema. Then up the narrow path leading to the many steps that lead up to the St Michaels Church graveyard before entering the Church. After church they walk home in the reverse, then after lunch, Mr D often takes the boys on a day trip, though mostly local as he would make several trips to fit everyone in the green and white Volkswagen T2 Caravanette. These are the day trips the boys often look forward to as a way of getting into the open countryside, different beaches and parks.

Summer holidays will soon be approaching and the one thing Derek is missing more is being at Cubs, something he has always looked forward to going to every week, missing the fun he had with his friends from Eversley as well as the new friends he made whilst he was there. He asks Mrs D about it, but she outright rejects his request. Although he's having a good time at the home with most of the boys he's now made friends with, it's the activities and skills that he was learning at Cubs he's missing more.

Chapter 25
Butlins

Summer holidays are finally here. His first one at Redhouse, and the one he's been looking forward to since seeing the photos in the brochure. Everyone is packed and ready for the long journey from Musselburgh to Skegness. Butlins is the destination and everyone is excited as they're about to leave for the next two weeks. The journey begins. A full Volkswagen T2, followed by three cars. One driven by Dingwall, one by Miss Murray and the third by Mr Nixon, who is part of the staff though not always around. They all set off on the long journey to Lincolnshire for the long seven-hour journey early on Saturday morning. Most of the boys sleep throughout the journey with a few rest breaks along the way. It's Derek's first time leaving Scotland at least in his mind as he's not aware he was actually born in London and move to Scotland six weeks later.

The convoy finally arrives at Butlins. As he looks around he realises it nothing like the tranquility of the Culzean castle woods that hosted the little white cottage and two caravans he's always been use to. There's a lot more people with rolls and rolls of chalets that look exactly the same line after line. It's easy to forget which is yours.

Everything is unloaded and carried to each of the chalets. The home has several on the same line. If the neighbouring holiday makers think they're getting a quiet fortnight, they're in for a shock though as England are still at school, it's a lot quieter than it would be. Derek is assigned to the chalet Miss Murray is in. She takes the double bed in the main bedroom. Two boys share the bunk bed in the second room, whilst Derek and the remaining two share the sofa in the lounge which is open plan with the kitchen. Looking around the chalet, Derek couldn't help but notice the colour of the bathroom suite. It's light blue, he's only ever seen them in white so stands out as unusual.

The Holiday pay is also good. Derek receives 50p per day. Everything in the holiday camp is free so he only pays for sweets and toys. Just a few days into the holiday Derek buys a postcard and asks Miss Murray for a pen. She sees the postcard.

"who's that for" she asks,

"my friends at my old home in Glasgow" he replies,

"right ok" is her response,

"have you got a stamp" she asks,

"what's that".

"you'll need one to send the card" she replies,

"wait".

she says as she goes into her room returning shortly after handing him a pen and placing a stamp on the table. He writes on the postcard then she returns as he finishes.

"Do you know the Address" she asks,

"Aye" he replies.

"your writings terribly, I'll write the address for you".

she says taking the pen from him then writing the address down as he tells her. She then licks the stamp carefully placing it in the square box at the top of the postcard.

"You just need to post it now" she says.

With the postcard ready, he goes running to the shops where the postbox is located. Everything is fine till the next day when Mrs D call's Derek to her Chalet. Mr D is there as he arrives. He has no idea why she's called him until Mrs D asks for the postcard,

"I posted it" he says,

"who says you could post it" she asks,

"Miss Murray helped me" he replies,

"Miss Murray is not in charge, we are" she says,

Then without a moment to waste, she tells Mr D to do it. Derek looks over to Mr D noticing he has a belt in his hand, he walks over to Derek grabbing him by the neck and pulling him down to the floor using his legs to clamp his neck as he thrashes his behind with the belt. He lets him go when he's finished. Mr D doesn't look at him, he looks away as Mrs D tells him he'll get no pocket money today and will remain in his chalet for the rest of the day. He leaves and returns to his chalet, Miss Murray looks at him,

"I'm sorry" she says as she cooks.

Derek couldn't understand what that was all about, just sitting contemplating what he did wrong and why sending a postcard was such a bad thing.

He sits in the chalet with nothing to do, listening to the sizzling pan coming from the kitchen area as Miss Murray cooks. The only time he sees the rest of his roommates is lunchtime, teatime, and when they comeback after the evening performances. At the home he wouldn't have minded, but this is eating into his two weeks of fun, with pain on his backside all over a postcard, that just said "having a good time in Butlins".

The day after everything is back to normal. Mr Nixon is out with his 8mm cine camera glued to his hand constantly filming the kids then having occasional showings in the TV room back home on his projector. Apart from Derek's painful incident, he leaves Skegness with happier memories.

Chapter 26
The Grove

Of course, that's only the beginning of the Summer holidays. The first two weeks are over but there's still a few weeks left. This week they stay at the home and wondering around the town is on Derek's mind that particular week. Again, visiting the harbour only keeping off the wall this time and spending time on the swings and beach at Fisherrow park only fills part of his time. There's much exploring to be done. A walk up Newbigging into Lewisvale park on the trampolines for a few pennies, then back down the same road with his eyes automatically clocking on to the huge Esso billboard fixed to the wall before hitting the High Street, then back home. He takes a different route next day. He chooses to go in the opposite direction along the river Esk. He walks along the path under the road bridge then facing the old roman bridge which is closed to the public, but not to the investigatory intents of a nine-year-old kid. Over he goes finding nothing to excite his imagination so he turns back over the bridge then carries on along the path listening to the singing birds the sound of the river flowing over rocks and fallen branches as he walks deeper into the Grove. Where does it end he wonders? As he continues along the path he hears the voices of other kids in the distance, but with a lot of overgrowth, he can't see who they are with the overgrown vegetation dominating the sides of the path along the way. The voices are getting closer as an opening appears. The first thing he sees are a set of clothes laid flat out on the grass on the other side of the river which seems to be just grassland before coming into view of three boys on a rope swing with one of them sitting curled up against the tree that supports the rope swing in his underwear. The other two are swinging in turn on the rope swing.

"dinni worry abute him, he fell in".

one voice shouts over laughing, though the curled-up kid doesn't seem amused,

"dae ye wanna go" the voice shouts again,

"aye" Derek replies,

"come over" he says,

Derek looks around,

"you'll have tae come over the bridge dune there, or swim over".

pointing in the direction of the Roman bridge.

"It's too far" Derek replies,

"it's up tae you."

Derek decides to carry on with his exploration. He already knows he gone too far, but just as he's about to turn back, he sees steps to his left and decides to do a little more exploration. Up he goes, as he gets to the top, he sees a stone wall, he's just tall enough to see over it, and recognises the building over to his far right across the field. Its the Kirk, and the wall divides him from the graveyard wall just over the field from the Grove. He also realises it's a short cut home, so climbs over the wall across the field climbing over the graveyard wall, walking through the graveyard path to the steps, that will lead him back to Redhouse. As he walks through the streets it not hard to pass a house with open windows or doors with the sound of the Scotland football teams World Cup song blaring out, eventually finding his way home.

A week later it's the second holiday away, this time they're going camping. Tents are loaded up, and the journey to their second location begins. Burrowhead campsite on the southern tip of Galloway is their destination. The convoy arrives at night and tents are pitched in the dark. The only evidence that the sea is nearby is from the crashing of the waves against rocks, and the glistening of the sea from the clear moonlit sky. There's too much excitement from Derek and his mates to sleep that first night, so to kill time, war begins in their sleeping bags as their legs commence battle play fighting, waving their feet inside their sleeping bags up in the air falling on each other only to be shouted at for the noise. Next morning it's bright, sunny but breezy. Derek gets up and looks out of his tent realising the glistening waves from the night before only told half the story, as its only now he realises he's camping at least a hundred feet above the sea on top of a cliff. A quick change, breakfast then off to the toilet block to wash before exploring his surroundings. With a few friends, he makes his way to the cliffs edge, but gets on his stomach slowly crawling forward. He's not forgotten the incident a couple of years earlier making him wearier of heights. Now close to the edge looking over, he sees the waves thrashing against the con-caved cliffs base. White foam appears as the receding waves fold with the noise deafening as they strike the cliff walls. Unlike the Butlins trip, this is to last only a week. There's little in entertainment with the exception of the clubs where some of the older boys sneak into with the added screening of the World Cup, but despite the sea being right on the site, they would need to travel five miles to access it. After a week the holiday is over and the boys are back home for the remainder of the summer holiday.

Chapter 27
Burgh Primary

Derek's first summer holiday at Redhouse is coming to an end and School is about to restart. As much as he's enjoyed his first summer, he hasn't forgotten how his last summer was and is thinking about his friend Frank, wondering how he is, hoping he's fully recovered.

Now back at school, there's not much difference to his last term before Summer with the exception he's in a new classroom, class 5. The class has a variety of characters. Kieth Mitchel who then what would be considered the class clown, though not in a bad way, he's intelligent but mischievous and funny always putting on a show, a bit like Peter from Eversley. One day he brought a golf ball into school tearing the outer skin before taking the elastic ball apart not realising the inner core of the golf ball is liquid filled causing the white liquid to spatter in his face as he reaches its core.

Alistair McGovern, the opposite to Keith, but again Intelligent, fairly quiet, but mad about football often spending his evening and weekends outside the playhouse near his home kicking his ball against the wall. Though Derek has no interest in football, he would join with him occasionally. The twins, Helen and Janet Veitch, not identical but similar in their ways, polite, friendly, and always wanting to take part particularly in anything Derek's involve with. And the others each with their own personalities that adds to the make-up of the class Derek felt at ease with being able to get through his remaining primary years.

Derek liked his school. Even though he knew he's not academically bright through those years, he found solace in how he was treated as a person. Both at school, at the home, and from those disassociated with the home that he came to know. One particular person Mrs Collins would play a major part in Derek's thinking through his remaining childhood.

As autumn hits with daylight hours shortening, the streets begin to fill with autumn coloured leaves as they fall from the trees. Soon, they expose their naked branches as the cold takes hold. The mornings become white with frost revealing a beautiful iced up spiders web on the gates to the yard of Redhouse catching Derek's eyes as he leaves for school. It reminds him of the cutout snowflakes he often made at his previous school, but this is nature's art, and far more beautiful. As he continues his journey, he takes more care avoiding the frozen puddles notable by its stillness in the wind as the mirror like surfaces reflects from the black tarmac that lies beneath. It's just another school day, but each with its own unique story.

Guy fox night arrives and Derek is on his way with the rest of the home to a firework display. As they arrive the fire is already lit. It's huge. Even at the distance they stand, the heat is felt though the cold night. Derek feels the heat on the front and left side of his body while the cold air takes hold to the right and back of his body. With the fire blazing the fireworks begin. Bang, bang, pop, pop, wiz, wiz, different sounds to each of the fireworks, till disaster strikes as one rogue fire work goes straight into the crowd further down. The show staff are racing over in a panic. It's difficult to see what's going on as Derek is further along the same line, but mouths are covered from those opposite the incident area, then turning to smiles and chitchat as news of no one being hurt circulates. The display continues with no further incidents.

On Memorial Day (Sunday), the boys are taken to church. Usually they sit downstairs with the balconies empty. On this particular day they're sent upstairs to the balcony. The church is full as the service is about to begin. A brass band can be heard coming from outside. It gets louder as they get closer to the church with the sound echoing through the large doors from the drum beat as men in various uniforms walk down the central isle followed by Cubs and Scout. After the service, and as they make their way back to Redhouse, Derek takes this as an opportunity to ask Mrs D again about joining the Scout group, and again he's denied.

Chapter 28
Christmas Home

Excitement fills the air at red house as Christmas approaches. The boys are excited. Derek can't see why. He sees Christmas just as he's done since he can remember. Boring with cheap rubbish gifts. A stocking full of chocolate with everyone leaving for a day or two, and now no Moreen to take him for the day which was the only thing he did enjoy about Christmas. Mrs D calls Derek to the dining room. He stands by the window ledge that divides the dining room from the TV room. There sits a paper and pencil,

"write your Christmas wish list" she says,

Derek looks at her bewildered. She looks back,

"go on" she says,

still he stands there, staring at her confused and bewildered.

"have you never written a wish list" she asks,

"no" comes his reply,

she explains it to him, then again asks him to write. He's reluctant fully aware he has problem with writing, but then tries,

"Thats the worse writing I've ever seen. Your spelling is atrocious"

she tells him taking the sheet and crumpling it up placing

another sheet on the sill this time writing it herself. And now with just a few days before Christmas the tree is going up. A real pine tree in the TV room by the window. The fairy lights are being tested plugged into the table lamp placed on the floor with 3 sets being used. In between each test, Derek puts his fingers on the terminals in the lamp holder. Within a few seconds he feels a shock, though not understanding what it is and not feeling actual pain, he sticks his fingers in again getting the same feeling. At this point Miss Murray has clocked her eyes on him.

"DEREK NAVSA"

With that being the only real shock, he jumps quickly moving his fingers away from what is about to be his third attempt, she continues.

"get away from there before you get fried".

Everyone looks at him as he gets up and walks over to the piano on the other side of the room.

"Stay there" she says,

Mrs D asks what happened, but Miss Murray lies to her saying.

"he nearly put his fingers in the lamp holder".

of course, she watched him do it, but most likely wanted to protect him.

It's Christmas Eve and everyone is called to the TV room. Each boy is handed an empty football sock and told to hang it on the line across the fireplace. One by one up they go then sent to bed. For Derek this is different from what he's been use to prior to Redhouse. He follows his fellow homeboys as they head for bed, though not much sleep goes on as the excitement of the next day is felt amongst the others. Not so much for Derek. He expects them to disappear for the day with him left as usual with a staff member. Not something to look forward to, particularly as non are equivalent to Moreen, especially Mrs D. Next morning Mrs D wakes everyone up going from room to room. With their dressing gowns on, they all head downstairs. Derek follows, but unlike normal mornings there's a rush.

"why the excitement",

Derek wonders as he follows. The rush ends in the TV room. Derek enters. There's thirty-two black bin liners spread out full to the brim, each with a boy's name on it. Derek walks over to his.

"wow" he says.

this is different. He takes each item out. Board games, books, "ironically" probably a piss take, but there's more. A post office set. As he gets to the bottom, he strikes gold. The thing he asked for is right there. The evil Knievel set as seen on TV, and far more to remember.

"Oh yes!"

"I asked for this!"

"yippee!"

and many other words from the excitement amongst the other boys as they too draw each item from their stash.

"Derek"

Mrs D calls him, distracting him from investigating his loot,

"get your stocking from the line" she says,

he walks over noticing the bulge in the huge football stocking he put up last night. Inside there's fruit, chocolates, and bits and pieces but nothing as exciting from that he was drawn away from, and too excited to remember if there was any breakfast. As lunchtime approaches, all the boys are instructed to change into their Sunday clothes. At that moment it's suddenly dawned on Derek everyone's still there. No one's left for the day, all still remain in the home having Christmas together. He goes with the others to change into his Sunday clothes as instructed. It's lunch time the boys now dressed make their way downstairs. As they pass the dining room, they notice nothing is laid out. No plates. No cutlery. Nothing Just empty tables. They head to the TV room, there waiting for them is Mr and Mrs D, Dingwall and Miss Murray. All too dressed up, though you wouldn't think it with Dingwall who always seems to wear the same clothes. Mrs D directs who's going in which vehicle and as usual, Derek ends up in the Volkswagen T2, though no complaints as he likes the caravanette. With everyone in the vehicles, they set off in convoy just like the two summer getaways only this time they're heading into Edinburgh, then into a restaurant which is empty with just the home boys. Clearly a pre-organised event. There's not much waiting as everything is already set out including crackers. Food is served almost instantly on the one long table which all are now sat on using both sides of the table, with just two waiters. Christmas lunch is served. It was kept as a surprise from the boys, but an enjoyable time. Lunch is over, bellies are full, and now it's time to head back home. Now all spread out with their gifts, using the play hall, TV room and the odd few in the dining room. Then the day begins to end. It's dinner time, still with a Christmas theme, after which the Christmas movie. A John Wayne movie before the night ends. It's his best Christmas Day so far.

On New Year's Eve, all the boys are sitting in TV room watching a late-night black and white movie still with a Christmas theme. At some point Derek is falling asleep. It's already 10pm and way past his bedtime and the latest he's been up since the night he was rushed to hospital with his swollen genitals.

"go on, go to bed".

a voice mumbles as he is half into his sleep. He feels his side being poked,

"Go on, get to bed".

It's Mrs D. He gets up and heads for bed missing his first New Year's celebrations, though he's not gutted as he's never experienced one and is too tired to stay up anyway.

It's now 1975, a month away from his first birthday at RedHouse before Derek turns ten. Day trips are generally limited in the cold winter months. But the toy shop Peterson's provided much entertainment in the form of toy cars and airfix models etc. Often Saturdays, Derek will visit Peterson's with his 50p pocket money buying either airfix models or matchbox cars, sitting in the TV room glueing the pieces together or playing with his cars often joining and sharing with Brian. Of course, with a house full with 32 boys there's always something happening that keeps them occupied.

Chapter 29
Mrs Colins

At some point as the boys get older, it's time for them to leave. On this occasion it's Tom Reid, or Tam, as he's known to his friends. He's the Brother of Robert Reid, the boy Derek had his first encounter with at Redhouse. And he too sleeps in the same room. He's leaving to join the army. His bed is now empty though not for long as Joe is moved into that bed, this is Derek's worst nightmare. How could he ask not to have him put in as he had already been threatened by Joe. From that day he made sure he did not go upstairs alone. Leave the room last if Joe was there. Often checking his whereabouts before going upstairs. He wanted as least contact with him for his own safety. But determined not to allow him to ruin his life.

It's Tuesday and as Easter approaches Derek is introduced to an old lady. She's in her late sixties and appears to be a regular visitor to the home. She takes him to her bible classes just around the corner from Redhouse by the river Esk where he meets a few of his classmates. The twins Helen and Janet, and another girl Lynda all three from his class at school. It's through this he gets to know all three girls more, becoming more friendlier with Lynda as he occasionally visits her at her home being welcomed by her parent. Mrs Collins is strong in her beliefs and has a heart of gold. Often she takes Derek on her fundraising activities and conventions as part of her membership with Christian Endeavour. And many weekends to her ground floor flat on Delta Road. She could walk for miles without rest, but more importantly instills values into Derek that shapes his thinking. A month after their first meeting, Mrs Collins takes Derek to her flat for the weekend. She has a one-bedroom flat. On Saturday morning as he awoke, Mrs Collins asks if he would help her light the fire at her bed ridden neighbours flat.

"yes"

is his reply thus before breakfast both go. Derek is introduced to Mrs McDonald as her dog jumps up at Mrs Collins. She then shows Derek how clear and clean the fireplace of its previous days burnt out coal, how much coal to place in and set the fire lighters to have the best results, then how to light the fire. He tries it and has success first time. With the fire now lit and the guard placed over it. Mrs Collins grabs the dog's leash and places it on the dog's collar.

"I'll be back shortly with your breakfast".

she tells Mrs McDonald in a slightly loud voice as her hearing is not great as both leave the flat with the dog.

"would you like to take him for a walk" she asks,

"yes" Derek replies,

And off they go across the field over the roundabout into the racecourse. The home had banned the boys from going near the lagoons, but Derek takes this as an opportunity to defy that order and walks the dog by the lagoons. With nothing there that looks dangerous, he's baffled as to why they are banned. After a while his stomach is telling him breakfast is ready. He takes the dog and returns to the flat where his breakfast is waiting. Mrs McDonald has already had hers. After breakfast Derek returns the dog to

Mrs McDonald. Later Mrs Collins takes Derek with her along with collection boxes to collect money for the RNLI Royal National Lifeboat Institution. A charity she strongly supports. Whilst out, a brief visit is made to Lynda's house whose parents are close friends of Mrs Collins before returning back to the flat. Next morning Sunday, Mrs Collins wakes Derek up asking if he'll go and light Mrs McDonalds fire and take the dog for a walk.

"yes" comes the reply,

doing exactly as instructed but not for those reasons. He enjoyed helping the old lady and taking her dog for a walk, just as he enjoyed helping Mrs Collins with her fund raising. Why is something he often asks himself, but always felt it was the right thing to do. After returning with the dog Mrs Collins has a brand-new set of clothes laid neatly out on the bed complete with a tie.

"It will be church time soon. I bought these for you".

she says,

"Thank you" he replies,

she leaves the room closing the door behind her telling him she'll have breakfast ready for him when he's ready. He walks into the Kitchen dressed in his new clothes.

"You look smart".

she says as she puts his breakfast on the table then placing a napkin over his shirt fearing he'll spill egg yolk over his new clothes.

"I usually go to the church on High Street, but for today we'll go to the church just down the road".

she says as they walk out the door. They return after service and Derek changes into his normal clothes as Mrs Colins folds the new clothes and puts them in a bag.

"you can take these home with you" she says.

"Thank you" he replies.

As the afternoon draws to a close, Mrs Collins walks Derek back to the home. Derek has never seen her travel by bus even though her home is just over a mile from Redhouse, she just seems to enjoy walking, and she's certainly not a slow walker. Derek often struggles to keep up with her.

Chapter 30
RAF Leuchars

Easter holidays are here and Mr and Mrs D takes some of the boys on a weekend caravan trip to a caravan site near RAF Leuchars. The site is pretty remote with a small river just over the cow field by the trees which are few in numbers. The caravan is an eight berth with a chemical toilet, but the boys are told to use the main toilet block. The fields adjacent to the site are owned by the caravan site owner and is a working farm often stinking of cow dung first thing in the morning. The field is supposed to be out of bounds, but the site owner is ok with them going over to the woods as long as they don't cause any damage. The caravan is similar to that which Derek went to for his caravan holidays whilst at Eversley though without the beach and the smell. This site also has a play area within the grounds, swings etc, though the boys prefer to mess around it the woods across the field which has a stream running through it, and is far more popular with the boys. But what really grabs their attention are the fighter jets often flying around the area as the boys try to figure out where they're coming from. The boys are called over for lunch which is usually sandwiches and soup when at the caravan. After lunch they're packed into the van ready for an afternoon outing. The destination is St Andrews not too far from the site. Whilst on the road, the location of the RAF airfield where the planes are from is revealed, but not without the life of them almost being taken out of them. From the road the airfield is not visible as there are hills surrounding it, but as the van is crossing the bridge of the river Eden, a low flying fighter jet flies over the roof of the van causing all to almost jump out of their seats. They watch as it flies across the waters then out of sight behind the hill landing. And though the runway isn't visible from where they are, it's obvious it's there. They continue their journey into St Andrews. Even though it's Easter, the temperatures are what you would expect during the early part of summer, a hot sunny day with little wind. It isn't a long journey and they arrive and park up ready for their Saturday afternoon exploration of the area. The van parks near the golf course away from the town itself. The walls surrounding the town look like castle wall and are visible looking over the large grass area. The boys spend most of their time by the beach, but a few including Derek decide to explore the area. It's not long before they come across what is probably the golf club house given it sits in the golf course. Seeing the TV on in the lounge, the boys stand near the door as it starts to cool down trying to watch the cartoon wacky races. It's not easy to watch with old folks walking back and forth until one smartly dressed old man walks over to them inviting them in to the lounge to watch it, then bringing biscuits over for them to eat as they watch the TV. It's much warmer inside as they grab the biscuits as if they've never seen them before though it is very rare they did get biscuits.

"Come on, we're going".

a voice comes from behind sometime later. It's one of the other boys who's come to find them.

"are you allowed in here" he asks,

"aye" says Derek, adding.

"the man said we can come in, and he gave us biscuits",

The boy looks around to see if there's any left as the boys get up heading for the door, sadly for him there aren't any. They make their way back to the carpark heading back to the caravan site as darkness falls.

Next day they're all up bright and early. There are no outings planned for the day as the D's are cleaning and packing, so the boys take advantage and set off to find the airport. Finding the bridge is easy as it's a straight road outside the caravan site. The walk is lengthy. As they reach the bridge, they take a left walking almost the same distance before seeing a plane crossing their path ahead. They realise they are close but need to climb a verge. Up they go now in full sight of the airport with the runway heading directly towards them. The fence is wooden, typical farm style fence up to Derek's chest,

"come on, let's sit on the fence" one boy says,

and without hesitation they do just that as a plane is heading directly towards them taking off. The full force of the sound doesn't hit them till it's directly above their heads. Their hands are fully raised up as if to touch the undercarriage but way too high for them to reach. The roaring sound from the engine as it passes over their head pushes them back, some just managing to hold on whilst others including Derek fall backwards over the fence almost rolling down the verge. With planes taking off every ten minutes and despite the deafening sound as they fly over, the boys shout from the top of their voice unable to hear themselves. It was the best ending to their weekend. On the way back to Redhouse, they stop at a fish and chip shop as it's getting too late and most of them are tired from the long walk earlier in the day.

Days later, Derek is woken late at night by an argument. Two boys are shouting at each other. It's Rab and Joe. Derek has no idea what the argument is over but picks the ending up.

"Come on, I'm taking you to Mr D" Joe says,

"come on then" Rab replies,

As Rab walks to the door he's followed by Joe. Just as Rab puts his hand on the door handle, he throws his elbow back hitting Joe in his stomach winding Him. He falls to the floor unable to breathe trying to gulp air. Finally after a minute he is crying in pain. Derek is covering his mouth with his bed sheets smiling at his demise, feeling no sorrow for him as his presence alone has always been torturous for him almost since he arrived at the home.

With just a month and a half before the Summer break, the boys arrive back from school one day as The warm weather approaches. There's something different in the yard at Redhouse. The T2 has gone and replaced with a blue ford transit minibus with all side seating. You could easily get more than the recommended backsides in that minibus and with most being small with a law that is pretty relaxed, that's exactly what happened. Though other vehicles were still used when needed.

During the May holiday, Derek is taken to a conference with Mrs Collins. Most of it is set in a church and they sleep at other local conference members houses close to the venue. On the Sunday coaches are laid on to take them to a huge park out in the open country. The field is huge and flat with a children's play area surrounded by huge hills. It's a sports day event for all the members and their families and Mrs Collins is one of the judges. As she goes to her base, she leaves Derek with the family whose house they are staying at keeping him around the play area. Derek plays there, but his mind is focused on the hill next to the play area as it's huge overshadowing the landscape. He wants to go up but is not allowed. He climbs on the bars in the playground but with his mind still on the hill he looses his grip and comes crashing to the ground. Luckily for him he has no lasting damage apart from a lump to his forehead and humiliation.

After he returns two new boys arrive at Redhouse. They are the youngest to arrive during his time and are put in the end bedroom above the dining room with it being the smallest room consisting of just three beds. It becomes known as the nursery, both boys are four and five years old. Mrs D calls Derek and tells him.

"we're moving you into this bedroom to look after those two",

Derek is not happy, but has no say so just follows her instructions, though in hindsight he's glad he's no longer in the same room as Joe. The two boys are fine, they sleep well and Miss Murray who sleeps on the other end of the corridor checks in periodically to make sure they're ok.

Chapter 31
Near Drowning

School has Broken up for the summer holidays and it's his second summer at Redhouse. The boys are packed into the minibus for Derek's second visit to Butlin's, only this time a much longer trip heading to Wales with Derek in the front seat between the two Ds, with Miss Murray following. The minibus barely leaves Musselburgh when Mr D slams the brakes causing the boys in the back to slide sideways towards the front of the minibus. Not because there is anything on the road. The road is clear. It's because the boys in the back are rowdy with excitement causing too much noise.

"Any more noise like that, and we'll be turning back".

Mrs D shouts. With that the journey remains mostly quiet. The journey is long, all 12 hours of it, and the reason they set off that Friday straight after School closes for summer. It's the most uncomfortable ride for Derek, he's having to sit with his legs sandwiched between a fat woman and a bulky gearbox that he isn't allowed to put his feet on, which would have given him at least some comfort. Their destination this year is Phewelli in north Wales. As they drive along everyone falls asleep, including Mrs D. The only two still awake are Mr D who's driving, and Derek who's in such a position he simply can't sleep. As they near Phewelli and drive along the hillside, the sea and town can be seen from high up where they pass. The holiday camp is on the other side of the seaside town, but the road they take goes around the town, so the drive is a slightly longer distance passing Phewelli to reach the holiday site.

Again like the previous year they all help unload the vehicles and are put into chalets. And again, Derek is stuck with Miss Murray, though he isn't complaining. She's not perfect and she does shout at times but she's ok, certainly nowhere near compared to Mrs D, and she has protected him a couple of times, however, he's also stuck in the same chalet with the two youngest boys, and it gets worse. Mrs D tells him he's not to let them out of his sight.

"where you go, they go" she tells him.

He doesn't mind helping out and doing his bit, but even for him, this is taking the piss. When does he get time to be with his friends and going around doing what he wants to do. Luckily for him, Miss Murray is understanding taking them when she's not cooking or cleaning. This of course will be the last Butlins holiday. Most likely because of the behaviour of some of the older boys. It's years later when Derek finds out this was the likely reason. As the week goes on, Miss Murray asks Derek if he would take the little ones to the pool,

"yes" he replies.

They take their swimming gear and head towards the pool,

"DEREK",

he hears his name shouted looking around trying to figure out where it's coming from.

"DEREK",

again, hearing his name then looking back. It's Miss Murray.

"COME BACK" she shouts,

"come on".

Derek tells the little ones as they turn back. Miss Murray walks towards them as they walk to her. She has two sets of inflatable wrist bands with her.

"here"

she says as she hands a pair each to the younger boys,

"ok, you can carry on".

she says as she heads back. Derek carries on making his way to the pool then helps them with the rings before going in the pool himself. He leaves them at the shallow end while he swims to the middle. He himself is not a strong enough swimmer yet to go in the deep end. He's keeps looking over to make sure the boys are ok, then watches as one of them gets out of the pool, sits on the edge then without warning jumps in. Derek sees him panicking. Even though he's got the arm bands on, he panics waving his arms about causing his head to submerge under water like a yo-yo. Derek quickly swims over, grabs him and pulls him out. He gives the woman sitting by the table nearby a look of disapproval as she sat watching it unfold and could easily have got to him before Derek.

"Don't tell Mrs D, please, I'll give you sweets" Derek tells him.

remembering what happened the year before when he got strapped and grounded. He knew perfectly well this would be far worse than a postcard being sent.

They stop at the shop on the way back keeping his side of the bargain, buying both of them sweets to keep them quiet before making their way back to the chalet only for the little git to blabber it out as soon as they get through the door.

"is this true" Miss Murray asks,

"No" he replies,

"He's lying".

Miss Murray asks the other boy,

"Yes" he replies.

Derek now realising he could be in deep trouble now looks at both boys not happy they grassed him up despite trying to buy their silence.

"Go Derek, have some fun" Miss Murray tells him.

He's confused but says nothing quickly making his way out in case she changes her mind. He meets up with others spending the rest of the day with them. Next day he's completely forgotten about the incident from the day before and goes to get his daily 50p from Mrs D along with the others. Derek notices Mrs D looking at him standing in the queue. He looks around checking to see if she's looking at someone else, she isn't, she's looking directly at him. Still he's forgotten about the incident the day before so found it odd she's staring at him. As soon as he gets to the front, he hears the dreaded words.

"Wait here" she tells him.

At that point he's remembered the incident. He becomes nervous. He looks at Mr D knowing he's the one who'll implement the belting, but Mr D looks at him not in a way he expected if he was in trouble. He doesn't seem angry but seems to be upbeat. Not the reaction he expects before a beating. He did get the feeling he wasn't happy beating him last year over the postcard, but this is different, the kid could have drowned and he knows he was responsible for looking after him. Could he be upbeat about beating him this time for good reason. This and all sorts are filling Dereks head with theories. Everyone has now had their daily pocket money, it's just Derek left still in his fearful thought, then a voice he's not looking forward to says.

"It's your turn".

He looks nervously at Mrs D.

"What happened at the pool yesterday" she asks.

"Nothing" comes the fearful reply.

"We know everything" she said.

With that Derek's worst thoughts are becoming a reality. Scared, he's now preparing himself for a repeat of last year. But then she comes out with,

"As a reward for your bravery, you're getting double today".

Derek looks at her utterly confused, he knew perfectly well he took his eye of the ball but wasn't going to both argue or incriminate himself. He has no idea what either Miss Murray or the boys told her. But he walked out of her chalet richer and happier. At least for that day.

Sometime during those two weeks the boys being boys just do what boys do and mess around. The funfair on some days remains closed till lunchtime. This particular morning it had been raining and the gates to the fair are closed. But the boys are small enough to fit through the gaps in the fence, and do just that, and it's not just the home boys, other boys from the site join them. With everything shutdown the boys discover they can move the carousel round just by pushing it. They all get on taking turns pushing it around. Derek decides to push it from the centre getting his leg trapped in the process. Luckily for him nothing is broken but he would bare the scars for life. Near the end of the Butlins holiday Derek decides to try out roller skating, he's never skated before and finds Haggis there though not on his own. For some reason, Haggis always seems to get lucky when it comes to girls, and is with not one but two. Derek put his skates on and he's clearly struggling to get on his feet. Every time he tried, he ended up on either his knees, back or his backside. Haggis is having a good laugh at his expense, but the girls feel sorry for him skating over to aid him. They grab him from both sides helping him around the rink teaching him how to balance and skate. After thanking them, they skate back over to Haggis. The last Butlins holiday finally comes to an end. The boys head back to Musselburgh and home.

Chapter 32
Runaway

After returning back to Redhouse, Mr and Mrs D go away for two weeks for their own holiday. Beardy bob and Miss Murray are left in charged. Still, it's the middle of the summer holidays and the boys just get on with their own thing. Derek often kept a distance from Beardy Bob. More because Joe always hangs around him. Both are in the yard along with Derek and a few other boys. Joe likes to try and push his luck when Beardy Bob is around and tries to approach Derek as he plays in the sand pit.

"Get lost" Derek tells him,

He gets closer, and as he's about to say something, Derek shouts.

"FUCK OFF"

This is clearly heard by all. Beardy Bob quickly goes over to Derek, and without any words slams his hand hard across Derek's face knocking him to the ground leaving him with the sound of bells ringing in his ears.

"don't ever let me hear that word again" he says.

Derek looks at Joe, he has a cheek-to-cheek smile on his face. Derek gets up and says nothing running straight out the gate. He runs to the top of Shorthope Street leaning against the one-way road sign for some time. A place he tends to hang around knowing if they were to come after him they would have to take the long route being as they can't drive up the one way road. After a while he climbs onto the flat roof of the single storey building further down Shorthope Street in sight of Red House. He stays there for a good while before walking away from the home back up Shorthope, crossing the main road then going through the arch that leads to his school with no food, clothing or even a jacket. He's now running away for the first time. He tried this a few years back at Eversley not getting beyond the front gates. This time he's gone and not just beyond the front gate, but beyond Musselburgh itself. Still, he's 10 years old and has no idea where he's really going and it's starting to get dark. It's late as he continues to walk. Even though it's dark and he has no idea what the time is or where he's even going, he's not scared. He manages to get just past Whitecraig before hunger, tiredness and the cold dark night hits him. He stops realising it's going to be a long walk to get back, and he's never walked a quarter of that distance before. The long walk has not only tired him out, he now has sore feet unable to walk any further. He turns back and does what he's seen done in movies, thumbing a lift. As luck would have it the first car that passes stops. He's totally unaware of the potential danger he could be putting himself in and runs to the car occupied by an elderly couple.

"Where are you going Laddie" the man asks,

"Home"

"Where's home".

"Musselburgh"

"What are you doing out here".

"Just walking".

"How old are you".

"Ten"

They weren't stupid, they clearly knew he's a runaway.

"Get in".

Derek gets in the car and they drive off heading into Musselburgh. The couple were being careful with their words not directly asking him why he ran away but asks.

"Have you been this far out on a walk before".

"No"

Continually talking to him throughout. They reach Musselburgh,

"Can you stop by the old town hall please" Derek asks,

"Do you live near there" the old man asks,

"Aye"

"I think it would be safer to take you to your house, it's not safe for someone your age to be out this late on your own".

"I'm ok I can walk".

"That's not a good idea, just guide me to your house".

Derek gives in and guides them to Redhouse. They stop outside.

"Are you sure you live here?"

"aye"

"It looks like a school" the old man says

"I live here".

His wife gets out of the car, walks through the gate and knocks on the door. Miss Murray opens the door, looks at the car then walks with the lady to the car. She opens the door,

"Come on, let's get you in".

Then thanks the couple who then drive off. Miss Murray takes Derek into the office,

"Sit there" she says,

pointing to the chair by the window next to the white phone. She makes a phone call from the other phone on the main desk. Derek doesn't know who she's speaking to though suspects it's the police as they turn up ten minutes later. Two officers walk in and sit on the chairs on the opposite side of the office.

"Where did you go" one says,

"Whitecraig"

"Who took you there".

"no one"

"You walked to Whitecraig on your own" he asks, as if surprised.

"Yes"

"Are you sure".

"Yes"

"Do you know how dangerous that was"?

"No"

"You're lucky the people you asked for a lift were good people, but it could have turned out differently" he said.

Derek looks at him with bewilderment, not understanding where he was going with all the questions. Not understanding he put his life at risk.

"Why did you run away".

"Mr Dingwall hit me".

"For what"

"Swearing".

"At him"

"No, at Joe"

"Why"

Derek wants to say, but he still fears what he might do and if they'll even believe him, so he just replies with,

"Just"

"Don't ever run away again, we had a lot of police officers out looking for you" he said,

Both then get up and leave. Miss Murray tells Derek to go to bed quietly. With that he leaves the office. A week later the Duncan's return. Mr D doesn't rush into dealing with the incident, but Derek is expecting to get his second belting. It's a few days later when he calls him into the office questioning him about the incident and the police time being wasted searching for him. Still Derek does not tell him what triggered the situation off despite having plenty of opportunity because he is still fearful. Mr D does what he did the last time grabbing him and pulling him to the floor again using his legs to lock his neck and thrashing his behind with the belt. He grabs his hands as he tries to defend himself with blow after blow raining down one after the other and unlike the last time, Derek can feel the anger from Mr D through the blows, this is far more severe than the last one. Eventually he stops. Derek gets up in tears. Another lecture is given, but he's in far too much pain to take any notice. The only words he does get is.

"Go".

With that he leaves the office, and heads straight into the

toilet cubicle sitting there for a good while just wanting to be on his own.

Chapter 33
New Dog

Summer holidays have come to an end and a new School term is about to start. He'll be in class 6. In a way he's glad to be back at school, more because he's around friends. As the weekend comes, Mr and Mrs D take a few of the boys in the minibus including Derek. They're told nothing of their destination which is not unusual as Mr D often takes the boys out without saying where they're going, so as far as they're concerned, they're going for a little ride most likely to a local park, however, that little ride gets longer and longer till they come to a farm somewhere out in the Countryside. They can hear a lot of barking as they approach a farmhouse. The minibus stops and Mr D gets out and walks around the corner. Not long after, he reappears waving his hand.

"Come on" he says,

The boys and Mrs D get out of the minibus, a rare smile is seen on Mrs D's face as they walk round to the sight of a fenced off area with several puppy Shihtzu Chinese Tibetan black and white dogs in it.

"Pick one" Mr D says,

The boys look around and look at each other wondering what's going on.

"Go on, pick one" he says again.

There's one dog that catches their eye and only because the dog stares at the boys.

"That one" says one of the boys,

No one adds to it or picks another.

"Is that the one".

They all agree. The two men discuss for a while then Mr D tells the boys to get back in the minibus as he leads.

"Are we no taking the dog" that same boy asks.

"Next week" Mr D says adding.

"He needs to be prepared before we can take him".

With that they make their way back stopping at a park along the way. A week later the puppy arrives and both dogs start interacting with each other instantly. The other dog is Sandy a golden Labrador that's been there before Derek arrived. The Shihtzu is named Shimming. Derek occasionally takes both dogs for walks, though even he is not immune from the teeth of Sandy. As the year goes on, the only thing on the minds of many in the home is the European cup next summer, and if Mr D's response to Dundee united losing a normal match is anything to go by, Derek can only imagine how he'll react if Scotland looses next year. Derek has no interest in football but even he can't understand why a grown man gets so excited and angry with guys kicking a ball around a field. Though occasionally the boys are walked up to the pitch near the racecourse to play football.

With the still warmer days, day trips become more frequent, particularly as all the boys can fit comfortably in the minibus for shorter journeys. One of the scariest day trips is to a place further north where the minibus is driven on a narrow two-lane road on what can only be described as a winding mountainous road. Mr D said

"We're driving on Devil's Elbow".

"It's bad enough holding tight onto the seat which has no seat belts fitted without the need to be told you're on a horror road", Derek thinks to himself. Even if the minibus went of the road, holding the seat would be of little protection. On the other side of it the boys spend the day surrounded by hills and mountains. They're playing in the valley. The wind can be felt rushing though the walls of the hills. As the summer sun hits four o'clock Derek along with some of the other boys decide to climb the hill, Mr D joins them. Up they go with some trying to run only to be defeated by the steepness as they tire out. Breathless, barely a quarter of the way up eventually slowing allowing the others to catch up. As they get just over halfway it's enough, they're all feeling the strain. Derek turns to see how far he's climbed to the most awesome sight that will be embed into his mind for the rest of his life. The broken clouds move fast with beams of sunlight float across the mountainous landscape as far as the eye can see where the distance fades with the heat rising from the wetlands, Mr D has now caught up, and the rest Join Derek taking in the beauty that only nature can offer,

"It bonnie"

The only words from Mr D, himself mesmerised by the living art show staring him. No one moves as they're just fixated on the the natural beauty in front of them.

"Come on, let's go".

Mr D says, with the boys starting to make their way down to a cup of soup and a packet of crisp before heading for home.

Chapter 34
Boy and a Chisel.

Mr D loves his woodwork. As a competent carpenter he's always working on projects within the home. His workshop is on the other side of the yard adjacent to the sandpit. Derek gets a rare chance to see the inside of it as he helps Mr D carry tools to the playroom. Part of the inside is similar to the woodworking classroom at the Burgh Primary school with a table purposely built with clamps. The playroom will be used to cut the wood for the new staff room being renovated along the corridor. Derek watches and at times helps as the frames for the walls and ceiling are cut in the playroom then put together in the small staff room to be. As work ends for one of the days, Derek is alone in the playroom with a piece of wood on the work bench with a very sharp wood chisel inviting him to try out which he does and with disastrous results. He tries to chisel the wood holding the piece of wood with his right hand and tries to shave it with his left hand being as he's left-handed. The chisel slips ramming straight into his right finger leaving a permanent scar. He tries desperately to hide the evidence but blood is already pouring from his finger. The cut is deep, he quickly runs to the toilets rapping his finger in toilet paper but the blood is penetrating. He takes it off and raps more over his self inflicted wound. This process carries on for some time until the blood slows. Now he has to hide the wound hoping he won't be caught. He pulls his jumper sleeve as far over the cut as possible to cover it now completely oblivious to the fact he's left a trail of evidence leading right to him as the D's follow his blood drops to the sink where he's just beginning to clean up.

"What on earth is going on here" she says.

Derek is startled by their silent approach and vocal reaction,

"Nothing"

"Where did the blood come from".

"I cut my finger".

"How"

At this point Derek goes into innocence mode making up excuses as only a 10-year-old could.

"Emm, I tripped over a piece of wood and my finger hit the chisel".

Of course, neither of them are buying it,

"So, you didn't try to shave that piece of wood clamped on the work bench" Mr D asks.

"Emm, No"

The evidence was clear and no amount of excuses was going to persuade them any differently.

Mrs D goes to him and rolls his sleeve up. He still has toilet roll rapped around the wound with blood penetrating.

"Come with me" she says.

She takes him through the kitchen into the sewing room

and pulls the first aid box out, then unwraps the toilet paper causing blood to restart. She takes him over to the kitchen sink and runs the cold-water tap.

"Keep your finger under that tap till I tell you to stop" she says

He does, then she returns after what feels like hours later,

"Take your finger out".

He does. The blood has stopped and she takes him back into the sewing room, dries his finger the puts a plaster over it.

"You can go now, but I'll deal with you later".

With that, he's pretty much certain he knows what's coming and he wasn't wrong, after an hour or two he's in the office on all fours, head clamped between Mr D's knees for his third belting. A week later a new boy arrives. Derek instantly notices he has a similar complexion to him though not sure if he's mixed race. Though in fairness, he himself doesn't realise he's mixed race. His name is John Suskis, same age as Derek and slightly shorter. It doesn't take long for them to become friends. John reminds him of Peter from Eversley, a sense of humour and loves joking around. He ends up in the same class as Derek almost instantaneous becoming popular with his classmates becoming close friends with Edward, or as he called him.

"Teddy Edward"

in reference to Edward Heath, who was prime minister.

John is from another childrens home in Largs the west coast of Scotland near Glasgow. Like Derek he spent most of his childhood in Children's homes, but never talked about the reasons why perhaps like Derek, he probably didn't know.

Chapter 35
A Night back to Eversley

Mr Black visits the home to check up on John as he's been there for a month now and is making sure he's settled in ok. At the same time he has a surprise for both him and Derek.

"How would you two like to spend the night at your last homes" he asks,

Neither of them needed to wait to respond. With excitement both simultaneously say

"Yes"

"you better get your pyjamas".

With that they both get in the car driving to Glasgow. Their first stop is Eversley to drop Derek off then on to Largs to drop John off. Derek arrives and will sleep in the same bed he slept in before he left. Most of his friends are still there but not Peter, he's left and he did not see Alastair or John but is told they're still there. He asks for Moreen but is told she's not been at the home for some time due to illness by a new member of staff who's been there since just after Derek left. He was hoping to see her but it's not to be. In the staff room which now doubles up as the TV room, his eyes clock onto the postcard he sent a year earlier. It's sitting on the sideboard and picks it up. He never told them of its painful journey.

He's playing with Alan and Frank, but they're not as upbeat or happy as they were when he lived there. Derek puts it down to them just being a bit older and more mature. He has no idea things are happening there and It would be twenty-seven years later when he finds out they were likely victims along with many others in that home of systematic sexual abuse, both there at Eversley and Downcraig after Eversley closed where the kids were moved to, the place where he could have gone had he not chosen Redhouse and most likely by the same man who told him about Moreen. Derek may have been spared the trauma of that experience, but his friends didn't, and after he heard of this it would haunt him not just knowing his friends were likely targeted but rekindled his own experiences of things that happened later in his own childhood. Next day Mr Black picks him up and takes him to Largs to meet-up with John. There, John introduces him to his friends. The place is huge, bigger than all three of his homes and is right on the sea front. They spend the afternoon playing before heading back to Redhouse. Shortly after their return, he's back in the attic, in the same room where he started and where his enemy is.

Tam Ried returns to Redhouse in his military uniform to visit his brother Rab. A commotion is heard coming from the Playroom. Derek goes in to find both are physically fighting each other and crying. Observing, Derek notices the punches are not forceful and couldn't understand why they would be crying. Having no relatives around him from the age of seven weeks old was to have a lifetime effect on his ability to show any kind of emotion towards family. He isn't aware that what he's witnessing in front of him is not cries of pain, but cries of love, bond, and emotions, that can only be felt by a close family bond. It would be years before he is reminded of that incident and get an understanding from one he would witness as an adult.

Sometime later during Summer, Mrs Collins takes Derek away for the weekend, not to her house but to her friend's farm out in the Countryside. The farmhouse is an old Victorian cottage, and once inside it's like time stood still. There's nothing modern in the cottage. It's like being on the film set of the railway children minus the costumes. Everything is Victorian. The clock, the Kitchen, the chairs, including a rocking chair, complete with an open fire. The cooker is coal operated and even the telephone is old. But as old as it is, Derek finds it stunning. Looking out the window is just a sea of green. In the distance a colourful array of trees as Autumn pushes its way in, with the hills forming a wave across the landscape. As darkness falls it soon becomes apparent that there's no electricity in this cottage as paraffin lamps are lit barely giving much light, Just a glow of orange flickering against the white painted walls.

"Things were not much different than this in towns and cities when we were your age" the lady says.

Derek doesn't reply but he's clearly fascinated by what he's seeing. His only hope at this moment is he doesn't have to go in the middle of field to relieve, but luckily for him, she does have one modern facility he can use.

After that interesting weekend, he's back at Redhouse and a couple of months later bonfire night arrives. Unlike last year, the boys don't go to a display most likely because of the incident that took place the year before, so Mr D bought a few fireworks to let of in the yard with a small fire in the sandpit. There are many things Derek disliked about the home, but the one thing he learns about Redhouse is unlike at his previous home, Mr D never compromised the safety of the boys. Mr D on one occasion told Derek he visits sites before taking them referring to Butlins and the camp sites. Most of the day trips locations, are those he already has knowledge of. Shortly after that night, one of the boys is leaving. Not for his age, but because he's moving to Australia with his family. Sat in a chair in the TV room, the night before he leaves, he's given gifts from the Duncans on behalf of the boys.

As his second Christmas at Redhouse arrives, like the previous year, the tree is put up in the TV room and with the football socks up all the boys are in bed. And as with last year, the boys are woken up early. This time Derek wakes up feeling wet. He looks under his sheets to find his pyjama bottoms are soaked. His bed sheets are also soaked. The rest leave the room, then shortly after a while Mrs D goes to his room to find him still in his bed.

"What on earth are you still doing in bed" she asks seemingly annoyed.

Derek says nothing still trying to figure out how he wet the bed. He's never done it before, eventually he tells her his bed is wet. Derek is convinced one or some of the boys played a prank on him, even Mrs D says

"it doesn't smell like wee", pausing for a bit before saying.

"it's probably just the excitement of Christmas",

Adding "go and have a shower",

It's not uncommon for Robert to play pranks on the kids,

and would be the likely suspect, though it didn't bother Derek too much, as he never got into trouble for it. Now showered he joins the rest in the TV room, and like last year, bin liners are full of gifts spread around the room. Derek doesn't need to look for his or read the name. It's the only untouched bulky bin liner left, and he heads straight for it. The radio is on and the Christmas number one is playing. It's Queens Bohemian Rhapsody playing as Derek begins to empty his loot. He asked for an action man and that's exactly what he got. As he digs further, he finds a cartoon projector. Not a real projector but a toy slide projector with cartoon slides. Though the only realistic place he's able to use it is in the Bathroom, and of course the other bits and pieces you throw into the back of your bedside cabinet never to see the light of day again. Christmas dinner is at the home this year with the tables laid out. It's not as elaborate as last year, but this was no disappointment for Derek. He's never forgotten the Christmas stays at Moreen's from his previous home. Neither has he forgotten his time with Alastair over two of those Christmases. But this is different. They're all together and that mattered because he no longer feels left out or alone. As New Year comes Derek is able to stay awake this time counting down as Big Ben strikes twelve, going to bed not long after.

It's 1976, and a month away from Derek's 11th birthday and he is finally given responsibilities. Most Saturdays till he leaves he'll be doing the shopping. For most kids, a boring thing to do. But not for Derek. He quickly discovers the perks of doing so. Not from the home, but from the shops he goes to with his shopping list. The only one shop he never receives perks from is the Butchers as there's not a lot that can be done with raw meat. From the groceries a choice of penny sweets. But his favourite is the Ice cream shop Di Rollo across the road from Brunton Theatre. Saturday mornings is when he goes to collect the large tub of Ice cream and given a free choice of a flavoured ice cream cone from the shop keeper's selection of ice cream out on full display on the counter. It's the one thing he always kept quiet, not sharing the information with any of his home mates, though he did suspect they were getting it free as he was always armed with note and no money, not aware the home had accounts with the shops. He gets the shopping done in the morning before taking his 50p then doing his own shopping in the afternoon. By late afternoon it's tv time for Cartoon Cavalcade at 5pm before the football results.

Not long after that, the TV room is closed and ready for Mr D's new project of upgrading the room, so for the next couple of months it's out of bounds to all the boys. The TV is moved into the Dining room in the far corner next to the glass panelled door dividing the tv room from the dining room, the grand piano also disappears never to be seen again.

Early that year Rab will also leave, leaving Haggis and Joe the oldest boys. But before he leaves, there's one more laugh to be had, and unfortunately for Rad, it's at his expense. As spring sets in there's a bird's nest on top of one of the pillars in the large shed next to the sandpit. Rab decides to climb it to see what's in the nest. Of course, the bird was in the nest and placed its butt over the edge of the nest dumping a load onto Rab's head as he gets halfway up, that sends him down with a mouthful of colourful words. Though he did manage a smile later. As he left new boys arrive, they're brothers one notably Willie Gallagher. Willie is from Glasgow, his face is disfigured after being burnt, but despite that disfigurement he was always jolly with a smile constantly on his face. As Derek gets to know him better he asks him about his accident and Willie is only too keen to tell him,

"I was playing near railway tracks a few years ago and got electrocuted".

Derek intrigued, asks more about it,

"Did it hurt".

"I woke up in hospital, I don't remember anything before that, but it hurt a lot. I spent months in Hospital and had to keep going back to get skin grafts done".

Derek questions him more,

"what's skin grafts" he asks,

"they take skin from other parts of your body placing it over the damaged area of my face".

Without any prompting Willie pulls one side of his jeans down showing Derek the scars on the side of his thigh where skin was taken from,

"Wow, it must have hurt while they were doing that".

"They put me to sleep but you feel the pain after you wake up".

Willie is not uncomfortable with the questions and is in some ways proud to share his experience, but sadly he would move back to Glasgow, later that year. That same year, and around the same time. Derek notices something missing. For months now, the tradition of walking to church stopped. No one seemed to know why, though it meant more outings. At the time it didn't dawn on Derek that some of the new boys are Catholic, with most of the others being Protestant. Perhaps that may have been a contributing factor but none of the boys seemed bothered.

Chapter 36
A Bloody Finger

Back at School Derek plays with his friends in the school yard. He's chasing one friend and gets his finger caught in the badge he's wearing on his jumper ripping the tip of his finger off. After being sent for first aid, it's decided he needed additional medical treatment. Mr D arrives at the school in his brand new Volkswagen Golf.

"hold your finger above your head and don't get blood on my new car" he says.

Derek complies looking at him knowing he's already got blood on his car door when Mr D closed it after getting him in, but there's no way he's going to tell him. As soon as he drives into the yard at Redhouse he gets out of the car.

"wait here and keep that hand up" he says,

He goes inside and a few minutes later Mrs D comes out, gets in the car and repeats Mr D's instructions to keep his hand in the air. She's a lot harsher than Mr D, so he moves forward to block her from seeing the blood on the door. She drives him to the surgery and as she gets out the car, Derek quickly wipes the blood on the door with the sleeve of his jumper just as she's walking around to open the passenger side door where he's sitting. He gets out of the car and she escorts him into the surgery. The doctor takes him in straight away, looks at it saying the tip of his finger is still there, but chooses to use butterfly stitches then using some contraption to put a bandage over his finger giving the same contraption to Mrs D with a supply of bandages.

Soon after, a new boy arrives at the home. One who is socially disconnected. He shoplifts and is pretty much a loner. Shortly before the Easter holidays, he's on his way to Musselburgh Grammar school. He's short for his age and would easily pass off as a primary school boy. He enters the newsagents before Derek then leaves just as Derek enters. There's two serving and Derek buys a chocolate bar. His favourite, a marathon. As he leaves the other server stops him.

"Wait there" she says,

Derek stops confused as to why she would stop him. She's still serving another customer as is her colleague who served Derek a moment ago.

"Empty your pocket" she says with no reasoning.

"Why" Derek asks,

"You've just taken something without paying for it"

Just as Derek it about to deny it the other server says,

"I've just served him; it was the boy who left just as he came in".

"Are you sure".

"Yes, he just bought a Marathon".

"Ok you can go" she says.

But it takes the other server to apologise to him. Easter arrives and Derek goes to Mrs Colin's for the Easter weekend. On Saturday morning he's not woken up by Mrs Colin's calling him. He's woken up by the neighbour's dog licking his face tail wagging like crazy wanting his walk. Derek gets up and as usual before breakfast takes him for his walk again to the lagoons and back. On Easter Sunday a similar thing, only this time when he sits at the table for breakfast his eyes instantly clock on to a small parcel neatly wrapped up like a Christmas present on the table in front of him with a tag. He's eating his soft-boiled egg whilst being distracted by the object. There's an envelope leaning up against the bread bin behind the little parcel, but he's too fixated on the object to notice the envelope has his name on it.

"You can open it after you've finished your breakfast" she says.

"What is it"

"It's a present" she says,

"But it's not Christmas".

"You can also have presents at Easter as well" she says.

He takes it and unwraps it to reveal what looks like a jewellery box.

"Go on open it" she says with excitement.

He opens it and there in the box is a watch, he takes it out having a good look at it. The face of the watch is silver.

"I'll put it on for you" she says.

Adding "I'll show you how to wind it up".

She puts it on, its Derek's first ever watch. He lifts his wrist looking at it for a good hour or so, he continues looking at the time almost every minute.

"That's from Mrs McDonald for helping her" she says,

adding, "Don't wear it all the time, only wear it on special occasions".

Allowing him to keep it on till he got back to Redhouse that evening.

The one thing that confused Derek that Sunday was the fact she did not go to Church, something he found odd given it is Easter Sunday. The day after he returns, the boys are in the minibus heading to the campsite near RAF Leuchars for the second Easter, though this time the boys spend most of their time sitting on the fence at the end of the runway watching the planes take off right over their heads. Never once did any official from the airport stop them. I guess as long as they did not wonder beyond the fence, they were most likely ok with it, and at a time where security was not really an issue they may have been at ease with kids passing time not being any trouble.

Back at Redhouse as the Summer months begin to kick in,

the school starts a cycle proficiency course after school. Every Tuesday for a few weeks two police officers took some of the kids on the course in the school yard. Derek along with two other boys from the home take the course. The boys first had to build up their bikes from the bunch of spares in the bike shed before walking them to school for the lessons. They're given strict instructions not to ride them until they have passed and in a strange way it's probably the only time they adhered to an instruction, though John Suskis thought having one foot on the peddle as it rolled down the path from school to the High Street wasn't riding. The day of the test comes and all of them pass with flying colours. Only Derek passes by what the policeman says,

"You passed by the skin of your teeth".

Derek looked at him and laughed saying.

"You don't have skin on your teeth".

Causing his colleague to laugh,

"Go on, get over there, you cheeky monkey".

He says pointing to the others at the start point near the girls entrance.

Now passed all three are now able to cycle back to the home. That same weekend Mr D decides to take the boys to the Sand Dunes at a place called Gullane beach just beyond Cockenzie, a favourite place for the boys mainly because of the sandy hill. The three who just passed their cycling test, along with another boy, who owns his own drop handle bike are allowed to cycle over. Mr D makes sure they oil their chains and check everything is working before letting them go.

Whilst the minibus is being prepared, the cyclists set off led by the boy on the drop handle who's also the oldest, heading off up millhill onto Linkfield Rd, riding past the racecourse over the roundabout then left heading straight towards Cockenzie. As they get close to Cockenzie, the minibus passes them to the cheers of its young occupants. The cyclists realise their regrets as they tackle the gruelling hill to reach their destination. They're relieved when they get there drinking plenty of water, the one thing none of them took on their journey. The Sand dunes is a great place. Beyond the car park it's just a mixture of sand and long grass to reach the beach which is below the hill they stand on. With broken hills and soft thick golden sand at the bottom. The challenges start, jumping off the verge to the soft sand below. Running down the sandy hill with sand flying everywhere being picked up by the shoes. Time was passing fast, and before they knew it, it's time to head back. The Cyclists on their bikes with a much easier downhill ride back. And again, overtaken by their cheering friends.

With Starkey and Hutch being the biggest thing on TV given they only have three channels at the moment, some boys including Derek buy little model paint tubs with their pocket money. They only buy two colours, red and white. Derek takes his cars and little vans out and paints them red with the Starsky and Hutch iconic white stripes. It doesn't matter which vehicle it is it gets the same makeover.

As the European cup gets closer, the TV is still in the top left corner of the dining room along with the table football whilst the TV room is still being revamped. Derek walks in drinking a can of Shandy he bought with his pocket money. Haggis is playing on the table football along with others with the record player playing in the background. Haggis has clocked on to Derek drinking the Shandy.

"you shouldn't be drinking that, it has alcohol".

"No" Derek replies,

"It has".

Derek not aware he's just drunk something he shouldn't have is speechless,

"You're going to get Drunk" Haggis says,

The others laugh. Derek never did get drunk. And if he did he was probably too pissed to know.

Chapter 37
A Lonely Old Man

At a time when danger was never an issue with kids. Or kids were just naive not aware of potential dangers around them, they would go beyond the boundaries that most would not some fifteen/twenty years later. Musselburgh is one of those places where crime was low. There's barely a time you ever hear a police siren unless there's a traffic accident. Doors are often left open with little fear of intruders entering. And risks were never at the forefront of the young kids minds. No-one to tell them of the dangers around them, with no such worry of "strangers", a word that they were never educated about, perhaps because of the times. Or there were never any incidents that warranted such a need. But that may well have been a false sense of security. Most people in Musselburgh are open armed, Derek always felt safe, so safe he never had the need to look over his shoulder when he's out on his own. On the Edinburgh side of the harbour, he would play with others from the home and with other local kids on the beach. Occasionally some kids enter a house who's back garden falls onto the beach for cold drinks. The house is owned by an old man and is always open. The old man is easy going. Derek himself also entered a few times. None were aware they could be putting themselves at risk. The old man seemed lonely and enjoyed the company and seemed harmless. It's possible he may have been related to one of the kids on the beach, but when Derek entered the house with a few others everything looked old. The grandfather clock is notable by the loud tick tock, and even though it's early summer and hot, he's poking at his coal fire set in a huge chimney breast. They sit there drinking orange juice from a real glass while the old man sits with a pipe in his mouth watching his colour TV. He never threatens anyone and the kids both boys and girls leave after the drinks.

With thirty plus boys in the home, it's not possible for all to have a bath in one go as there's only two bathtubs, thus all are given specific days when they have their bath, which is ones a week. But all have a shower on Friday night as there's enough showers. Derek's bath night is Thursdays which means after Friday he can't bath or shower for six days. All he has is his morning and evening wash in the lined up back-to-back row of sinks, where he's at least able to climb up to sit onto the back of the sink and wash his feet. On this particular bath night Mrs D decides to fill the bath, something she's never done before. Without checking to see how hot it is, she tells Derek to strip and get in. Derek notices the steam coming from the bath is far more than it should be and puts his hand in to check.

"Miss it's too hot" he says.

And it is, he could barely put his hand in with it being so hot,

"It's no hot, get in".

"But Miss"

She's not taking no for an answer. She picks him up while he's still in his clothes, and throws him straight into the hot bath. He screams out. She strips him whilst he's still in the tub. As she takes his T-shirt off, she instantly puts the cold water on. She panics but doesn't take him out or let him out. Though the water is not boiling, it's hot enough for his skin to turn red. With the water now cool enough, she leaves the room saying.

"Hurry up and have your bath".

With no apology for the wrong she knew she did.

The nights are getting longer, the daily sun is nonstop, it's exceptionally hot for late May. Many more outdoor activities and education is taking place at the Burgh School. Walks along the Esk. A visit to Bruntons. Police dog exhibit in the field at school. Bullying if any is rare at school, but the odd skirmish takes place even amongst friends. Derek, John Suskis and Ewan Slight would often walk home together. Ewan a classmate who lives just behind the home and also a friend of the two boys get into an argument with Derek. As they reach the end of Shorthope street coming home from School by the toilets adjacent to the bridge, both he and Derek's argument turns into a skirmish, both pushing each other raising their fists but not throwing any. It almost becomes a wrestling match ending as Ewan pushes Derek down the ramp next to Shorthope bridge almost ending up in the river. The river is not deep, and he only gets his shoes wet. As both go their separate ways, they do what all boys do, threaten each other completely forgetting about it the next day back to being friends. But these incidents are not only isolated to friends. Sandy, the homes golden Labrador is got to be the world weirdest dog. Often at the home the boys play fight, wrestle, use twigs to play cowboys and Indians, but Sandy can't tell the difference between a real fight and a fake fight. For many years Derek has been convinced Mrs D has trained that dog to do her dirty work. Because for some reason he alway tries to bite the boy's backsides when they're fighting, and Derek is no different, even though he takes both dogs for walks regularly, the daft dog still turns on him and bites his butt. Luckily he never bites hard enough to cause any damage. Strange animal.

Chapter 38
First Family Contact

It's Friday late afternoon and Derek is home from school playing outside in the yard. Shortly before Tea his name is called.

"DEREK NASDA"

It's Mrs D, she always called both him and Haggis by their full names as both have the same first name, but still after 3 years you'd think she would get his last name right.

"Run to the office, there's a phone call for you".

Derek is confused, who would be calling him, he's never had a phone call before, "perhaps it's Mr Black" he thinks. He runs to the office. Mr D is sitting at his desk pointing to the white phone by the window that's off its hook. Derek picks it up.

"Hello"

He says,

"Hello"

Comes the reply,

"I'm your sister Ann".

The voice is strange, not the English he knows, she's cockney. Derek looks at Mr D, confused, but he's not much help. He just looks at him with a grin.

"Are you there".

The voice says as he's so far not responded,

"Alan, I'm your Sister".

She says again using his original first name. He's struggling to respond, he can't, he's always thought his parents were dead and had no family and no one has ever told him he not only has a sister, but his parents are very much alive and that he has other brothers and sisters. For a while he lets her do the talking, listening to her as she tells him about his family in her strange accent, he talks little,

"What are you doing" she asks.

"Talking to you".

it's all to much for him not knowing what to say. It's his first time talking on a phone, they carry on chatting for a while then she ends the call by saying.

"I'll call you every Friday at the same time".

They say their goodbyes and Derek leaves the room upset, he was never warned or even made prepared for this. It was a complete shock to him. It's a whole load of new for him to take in. He goes to his room and lays on his bed just thinking about what just happened now with far more questions than answers. Why has he spent his entire life in homes? Why did no one come for him? Why did no one even visit him? Why was he stood under the clock every Christmas at Eversley, while everyone else's families came to take them and not him? And what happens now? A few days later Mr Black turns up apologising to him saying she wasn't supposed to call until he had spoken to him and explained everything. For the rest of his time at Redhouse, Ann stuck to her word phoning him every Friday at the same time.

All the boys are called into the washroom, two sinks are being used to comb and wash nits out of the boys heads, Mrs D on one sink combing with a nit comb while Miss Murray washes with some treatment designed to rid of nits. As Derek has his hair washed Miss Murray comments on his hair

"He has beautiful jet-black hair".

Derek with his head in the sink, only inches away from the water smiling at her comments, hoping he'll still be alive to enjoy it without being drowned.

With the long hot summer evenings, Derek regularly rides out on his bike. He usually rides to the harbour or the Grove. This particular evening he's riding to the Grove. As he rides under Bridge St, Bridge, he hears his name being called.

"Derek come here".

He looks back, it's Joe, he's running behind him. Derek speeds up,

"Come here" he shouts again.

Derek is not heeding his call riding as fast as he can with Joe still running behind him .

"When I get you, I'm going to kick your heed in" he shouts.

Derek now a good distance from him sees an opportunity to tease him by sticking his two fingers up to him and sticking his tongue out then smiling.

"I'll fucking get you".

He shouts again, still running. Derek rides into the Grove, as he gets in sight of the rope swing that's on the opposite side of the river, he realises the only way out, is the way he came in. If there's another way out, he's not seen it yet. He knows where the wall to the graveyard is, but he also knows he can't lift the bike that high. He starts to ride back, but slowly. As he turns the bend, he sees Joe.

"Fuck"

He says softly to himself. Joe has spotted him and starts running towards him again. Derek quickly turns the bike round riding further into the Grove. He waits for a while seeing if Joe is still following him. He already knows he's out of his comfort zone with this being the furthest he's been along the Grove and has no idea where it leads to. Joe doesn't appear so Derek slowly makes his way back stopping whenever he hears crackling of twigs from the overgrowth. He gets close to the shelter which looks like an old air raid shelter or something strange left in the bushes most likely forgotten about over the years which Derek and a few others from Redhouse use as a den. He expected Joe to be there waiting. He has two choices, creep along slowly or ride as fast as he can. He goes for it hoping for the best riding as fast as he can hoping to get past it without him noticing him only to be let down by his mudguards that are not on the same page as they're rattling loud enough to alert anyone. As luck would have it, he isn't there. It's when he's passing the side street on his right, he sees him running out from the corner of his eye, but he's still riding fast enough to get away from him.

With the hot Summer, day trips are increasingly regular. This time a trip to another seaside. It's windy but hot as they arrive. The sea is choppy. It's high tide and the waves are splashing over the sea wall. Some of the boys try their luck including Derek, standing behind a higher wall as the waves batter the walkways. Suddenly a huge wave hits the wall they're standing behind as what felt like three bath loads of ocean water comes over that wall soaking Derek and his other daredevil friends only to be told off by Mrs D which is nothing new. Mr D didn't care, he saw the funny side of it laughing and joking with the soaking wet victims of nature's one-sided water fight.

Chapter 39
The Floating Rock

Still hot, Derek spends more of his time in the park by the promenade to cool off from the sea breeze often sitting on the beach playing in the sand. This time is different. As he looks out at the passing ships in the far distance with views of the land across the river forth partially faded from haze across the horizon, he notices an object floating on the water as he pulls his eyes back to his location being pushed and pulled as the waves hit the sand and recede.

"What the hell is that".

He says to himself, there's no one else around him so he quickly walks over to the sea.

"It looks like a rock".

Again, saying it to himself. He tries to grab it as the waves pull it in then out, but he has no way of reaching it. He looks around for something to reach far enough to get it but there's nothing except for a couple walking along the promenade towards his location from the mouth of the river Esk. Now he sees getting the strange object as urgent,

"What if they see it".

He thinks to himself thinking they might grab it for themselves. He quickly takes his shoes and socks off, roles his jeans up and walks into the waves. It may be exceptionally hot, but when that wave hits his legs he certainly feels the cold. He's reaches it and picks it up. It is a rock but not any rock.

"How can a rock float"

Again, talking to himself. He hears a man's voice shout.

"WHAT IS IT" he shouts.

Derek looks back, it's the couple who are walking along the Promenade.

"ITS A FLOATING ROCK",

Derek shouts back with no choice as they are both at a distance.

"IT MIGHT BE VOLCANIC ROCK" the man shouts,

The man almost equally excited with his find starts to make his way with his partner down the beach. Derek's getting nervous. He grabs his socks and shoes and starts walking away from them.

"It's ok, don't worry I'll stop here. Can you show me the rock" he asks? Putting his hand up.

Derek stops and holds his hand with the rock up. They're not that far from each other now so don't need to shout so loud, and Derek has no intention of handing it over to him holding his distance prepared to run if he moves any closer.

"Do you know anything about it" the man says.

"No" Derek replies.

"That's an incredible find, it's rare to find something like that when that volcano has been dormant for millions of years".

Pointing to Arthur's seat, a rockery sloping hill protruding the landscape in the distance which last erupted as a volcano some 340 years ago looking beyond the harbour as he's seemingly surprised by the find.

"Wow"

Derek says quietly to himself realising its historical significance. The rock itself is just a little larger than a tennis ball and consist of tiny air pockets, light but not too light. The couple start heading back up onto the promenade leaving Derek to get a good feel of his find. Fascinated by its ability to float, he goes back to the water's edge putting it in and taking it out several times just watching it float. It's kept by Derek for many years after he leaves Redhouse until one day when it mysteriously disappears.

The TV room is finally finished, and the new layout is revealed to the boys. The TV that once sat in the far corner is now inserted into the fireplace with doors. A new carpet laid out and chairs all the way across the back wall where the grand piano once stood. A small side table is built next to the fireplace where clean socks are left for the boys to take up each evening to wear the next day. Each with the number of their wearer sewn inside each sock, like that of an infant school child's coat.

Chapter 40
The School Plant

A few weeks before the School year ends, Derek is offered the class plant. A cactus. It's a plant he's always liked, so when asked, he doesn't hesitate immediately saying.

"Yes"

With excitement he takes it home but Mrs D sees him with it.

"Where on earth did you get that from" she says,

Startled by her sudden question he said.

"The teacher gave it to me".

"Where're you going to put it".

Of course, he's worried she'll tell him to take it back or worse throw it out,

"In my room"

"How on earth are you going to look after it"

Derek is speechless, but what surprises him is how she responds. She may be a lot of things at times bitchy, cruel, evil, but it turns out she has a soft spot for plant. She loves them.

"You're no putting it in your room, follow me". She says

Derek follows her to the dining room as he carries the cactus to the window that divides the dining room from the TV room,

"Put it there" she says.

He does,

"I'll help you look after it" she says,

Derek is in complete disbelief wondering who this woman is standing in front of him,

"does this cactus have mystical powers".

he asks himself. This is not the woman he's known for the past 2 years, if only she had the same feeling for the boys. She kept her word and taught him how to look after the cactus making sure he watered it regularly.

It's the last day of School, and the school is preparing for sports day as the Summer holidays arrives. In pairs the school is escorted to Pinkie Primary School, it has the biggest field and can cater for the entire Burgh School. Derek is not the sporty type at school and doesn't take part. He still has to go and cheer his house, a name given to each of the years which ironically follow the names of the local areas, though not much cheering is happening as the kids just seem to play amongst themselves given the teachers are too busy trying to sort the teams out. As his house completes, the kids are free to leave. Derek and John leave together, not via the gate they entered but via the gate leading towards high street signifying the beginning of their summer holidays and the same entrance he will re-enter a month later for a local Highland games event.

Unlike the previous two years, there's no Butlins this year so there's no rush to leave. The first week is spent at Redhouse. Derek along with his three fellow cyclists ride around Musselburgh mostly through the grove as its more adventurous with dirt tracks and uneven surfaces. Whilst on the bike ride through the grove, they hear the sound of a pellet gun. The sound seems to be coming from the top of the steps where the graveyard wall is. They follow it dragging their bikes up with them as it's way too steep to ride. They find a boy older around fourteen or fifteen years old with an air rifle shooting at cans set up in a row. He welcomes the boys clearly recognising one of them from the home as he knew his name. He lets the boys try the gun out taking the time to show them how to use it and shoot. It's Dereks first time using an air rifle and he's clearly enjoying it. After several attempts he's able to hit the target. With the excitement they've completely lost track of time. None of them have a watch on and Derek is only allowed to wear his on special occasions.

"We need to go".

The lead boy on the drop handle says. They grab their bikes, thanks the boy, and make their way back down the hill rejoining the path. But rather than turning back, they continue on with their bike ride. Luckily for them, they didn't loose too much time when they returned back to Redhouse .

Chapter 41
The Nightmare Ends

A few days before the boys head off for their holiday. Mr D gets them all into the side garden adjacent to the dining room to help him erect the new tent that would be used for the holiday. It's a huge off-white bell tent. Teepee to some. A single pole with the canvas pegged out, with more than enough space for all the boys to sleep comfortably. That same weekend the boys leave for Clayton Caravan site near RAF Leuchars. This time for two weeks. From there they will travel to different places, and best of all a visit inside RAF Leuchars itself as there's an air display going on the following weekend. After arriving at the site, the minibus stops slightly down from the caravan where the tent along with most of the boys kit is offloaded before the minibus heads up to the caravan. Derek along with a few other younger boys will stay in the caravan. He would have preferred to stay in the tent, but given Joe is in there he's not complaining. With the tent up, the boys from both tent and caravan head down to the play area, though as usual one person is notably not there. He's most likely found some girl to hang around with, which is not uncommon for Haggis. He seems to have away with girls. Haggis has always been a tough cookie, scary at times and though he loves to mess around. For the boys, that will all change during this holiday. The weekend arrives and the boys are excited, or at least those who spent many times sitting on the fence at the end of Leuchars runway. For this time they will be going inside the airport itself and up close to the very planes whose fuselages were flying right above their heads, watching them doing manoeuvres they've only seen done in movies. Then to round off the highlight of their visit to see the Red Arrows with their colourful aerobatic display controlling the skies around them.

Just two days later Derek is finally relieved from his horrors of two years. He's by the caravan when he hears a commotion coming from the tent. The tent door is on the other side so he's not able to see what's going on. Mrs D is inside the caravan washing up completely unaware of what's taking place. There's shouting,

"GET HIM" shouts a younger squeaky voice,

Just then, Joe runs from the tent towards the field chased by Haggis and the others.

"GET HIM"

Mr D is nowhere to be seen. They all climb over the fence chasing Joe towards the trees by the river. Derek doesn't need to ask what's happened; he's already figured it out. He runs joining in on the pursuit. By the time Derek catches up, Joe has already been cornered inside the woods and held by Haggis. Moments later Mr D turns up and takes control.

It's often thought kids brought up in children's home are thugs and criminals. That's a lack of understanding of these kids many of whom have gone through the care system. They are there because some are vulnerable. There was a mob there with plenty of time and opportunity to do some serious damage to Joe. He did to the younger kids what no person should do. But they held back, as much as some of them wanted to beat him up, they didn't. Because they are just normal kids caught up in unusual circumstances, and like most kids they know the difference between right and wrong.

Joe is taken away from the site and by the time the boys get back to Red House, he's gone. But the ordeal has not ended yet. Police interview everyone involved, particularly those who were victims. Finally, Derek is able to get it off his chest telling them everything that happened. It is over now and he has nothing more to fear or does he.

Haggis became the hero. From that point he was looked at as the big brother, and the only one in the home gutsy enough to stand up to Mrs D.

The European cup is on, its Saturday afternoon and Scotland are playing. From the offset things are not going well for Scotland. The goalkeeper would become the fall guy for Scotland's downfall and even though Derek does not have much interest in football, it's obvious to him. During the entire game Derek is not focused so much on the TV as he's more focused on Mr D and his reactions to every failed catch. As the match goes on his name is called.

"Derek Nasda"

The voice is unmistakable, only one woman in that home in nearly two years still can't get his name right, and that's Mrs D,

"I need you to go to the Butchers".

She says with her hand stretched out with her shopping list even though there's just one item. Derek is lying on his stomach elbows to the carpeted floor folded up with the palm of his hands holding his head up. His legs from his knee down folded up, as its tight in the TV room. There are far more kids than chairs, and most need to cram together on the floor.

"Miss can I go after this".

He really means after the show Mr D is putting on. Just then the whistle goes off for halftime.

"If you run, you'll get back in time for the second half". She says

He gets up, takes the list with one item on it and runs out the back door, up Mill hill through Kerr's Wynd, through the arch then straight into the Butchers. For a Saturday afternoon the streets are quiet. No doubt everyone is at home shouting at their TVs like Mr D. It doesn't take long for the Butcher to cut meat given there's no one else there. He takes the bag and runs back to the home just in time for the second part of the Mr D show. Scotland goes on to lose.

A few weeks later the boys take their place near the old town hall for the annual carnival where floats of all kinds take to the streets starting from the racecourse running down high street then ending somewhere near Lewisvale park. A tradition that has been a focal point of Musselburgh for decades, and one the boys look forward to as a means of increasing their pocket money. This particular year Derek finds himself with a few others from the home on the Local news covering the event as they run onto the road as money is thrown towards them. Luck was not always on their side as it depended on where the coins were thrown. This time towards them despite getting told off by Mrs D, to them it's a risk worth taking. But it's not the only scramble they take part in. Often the boys including Derek will go to churches on Saturdays where weddings are taking place. There's a tradition where the married couple throw money as they exit the church after their ceremony. It's a scramble, and the boys are pretty much organised not sticking to one church. They spread out covering others if the times clash for maximum income. Of course, they don't share their grab with each other. There's never been a time when the boys are moved on, it's almost like they expect them to be there perfectly willing to throw their money. Perhaps they see the scrum as entertainment. Whatever their reasons the boys didn't care and would often thank the couple. And the boys would always find ways to entertain themselves, like the time three boys jumped in Derek's bed playing rollover, a bit like ten green bottles, but four in a bed singing then rolling over till one falls out, though with the last, the mattress is thrown over.

Derek spends a lot of time at Lynda's house using bed linen over the washing line in the garden shaped out like a tent. Riding along the pavement on bikes and around Windsor Gardens. Playing monopoly and getting in trouble for picking the rhubarb from the garden. Or just watching her pet Turtle taking its time walking slowly with no care in the world. Derek always regarded her as his sister, at times going on day trips with her and her family.

Chapter 42
The Headmasters Office

School restarts. The class are back together for their final year at Musselburgh Burgh Primary School, but there's nervousness as they are aware the teacher for there last year is Mrs Samuels. She's the strictest no nonsense teacher in the whole school. On top of that, she's the deputy head. They'll be in class 7, but as they enter the classroom, they find out it's not the teacher they expected. It's a fill-in teacher temporarily taking over for Mrs Samuels as she suffered a heart attack over Summer. The fill-in teacher is ok but she's only temporary. And for that duration the class is on the top floor facing the Gym hall. Derek is not doing well during this time, struggling as usual with almost every subject except Gym. It's got to a point where the teacher can't cope with him and sends him to the Headmaster. He stands outside the headmasters office waiting to be called in. He knows if you are sent to the head you're more likely to get the strap. He accepts that fate even though he himself knows he's incapable of changing his ways more because though he can read, he simply struggles with the characters in the words. Mr Borland the head calls him in.

"This is your first time in here isn't it".

"Yes"

He takes a book out and opens it at a random page.

"Read this" he says

Derek looks at it and starts reading, the headmaster stops

him.

"What are you seeing in the book".

"I don't know what you mean".

"Describe what's happening when you're reading the words in the book".

He looks at the book with the page still open where he was reading from.

"The letters are moving sometimes up and down or sideways".

"Does this happen a lot". He asks

"All the time" Derek replies

Everything goes quiet. The headmaster goes to his desk and starts writing notes. Derek tries to lean forward tiptoeing to see what's being written almost loosing balance, but can't see what he's writing.

"Ok Derek, go back to your class".

Derek looks at him confused slowly walking to the door. The headmaster smiles at him.

"Be good".

He says as he opens the door and leaves returning to his class. He never heard anything about it again. Shortly after, the class moves from the top floor, directly beneath to the first floor, as Mrs Samuels returns after her illness. She's deputy head always wearing robes, and strict, but it turns out she's not as strict as they thought, and at assembly she always plays the piano.

The dry hot summer ends with a bang. It's mid-August, and humid. Most of the boys are struggling to sleep and are sweating, on top of that there's a heavy thunderstorm. Despite the curtains being closed, the room fills with flashing lightning, with the noise from the thunder at times deafening and scaring some of the boys. Both Mrs D and Miss Murray are going from room to room checking on them, removing layers of blankets and opening the window, to allow air to circulate. Not helpful when it's the noise that scares them more. But a necessity where the humidity and heat is overwhelming.

For months Mrs D has been telling the boys who cycle to get bicycle clips. To often the boys return with either oil stains or tears on the ankle of their jeans as they either scrape against the chain or get them caught between the chain and cog. Derek goes to the shop with his pocket money asking for bicycles clips. The shop keeper hand him a set. Derek looks at him.

"Are you ok" the keeper asks.

"What are these?

"bicycle clips"

Derek stares at him as if he's been conned.

"You've never seen them before have you".

"No"

"I can tell by the way you're looking at me".

Pausing for a moment smiling,

"Let me show you" he says

He takes the clips from Dereks hand, crouching down,

"Bring your leg forward".

Derek complies. The shopkeeper starts pushing the clip over the ankle of his jeans.

"Ooh, what does it do".

"It stops your trousers getting caught in the chain".

Derek pays for them thanking the shop keeper for helping him then heads straight back to Redhouse. He shows Mrs D the clips.

"Good, make sure you wear them when you ride your bike".

"Ok"

Later that night when all the boys are in the TV room, she announces it to all giving him an extra 50p, which seemed a bit odd given only four of them are allowed to ride bikes.

Chapter 43
Mrs Mop

The home decides to have a disco night and the boys are told they can bring one girl. For Derek that's easier said than done as he struggles to say no to anybody. He invites Lynda his friend, but the information about the disco night soon leaks out and he's asked by other girls if they can go. He struggles to say no, so he also invites the twins Helen and Janet who asked. All three turn up taking turns to dance with Derek. He doesn't get into trouble as they saw the funny side of it, though he's teased by the other boys for a while after the disco. For Derek he's always had a soft spot for the three girls as he knows they like him.

Halloween arrives and Mrs Colin's invites Derek to a fancy-dress party. Mrs D suggest he should go as Mrs Mop. Derek has never heard of Mrs Mop and not aware of what it involves, but he agrees only to find out it involves him wearing women's clothes. The boys seeing him dressed like that are the least of his humiliations. Mrs Colins arrives to collect him,

"Are you ready Derek". She asks

"Yes" he replies

"Let's go".

Out they go, then out the gate. Derek looks around for transport, but there's none

"Are we walking" he asks

"Yes" she replies

"Can't we go in a taxi?

"It's no far".

"Where is it?

"The scout hall"

"The one just before your house?

"Yes"

"That's far".

"You've walked there many times".

"Not in women's clothes"

She smiles,

"Ah of course not but don't worry, no one will know".

As they walk up Millhill, Derek keeps his head down hoping no one notices him. They reach the racecourse continuing their journey.

"HELLO MRS COLLINS"

A voice shouts from the other side of the road where the houses are. They stop. Derek takes a quick glance over to see it's the mother of a girl from his school. They start chatting or rather shouting to hear each other. Her daughter is by her side. Derek panics not only because she might recognise him but they're also standing right outside Lynda's house. Derek faces towards to racecourse hoping she doesn't mention his name, she doesn't. Eventuality they part ways. Derek is relieved, the last thing he needs is being mocked at school. They carry on over the roundabout then straight past the Scout hall.

"I just need to get something from home".

She says as they turn the corner to her flat, which thankfully is the first one on the street. They make their way back down to the Scout Hall. The afternoon is spent playing games and doing all the stuff normally done on Halloween. There's a fair few kids there, Derek luckily doesn't know any of them and they don't know him, or at least he hopes they don't. The party continues for almost two hours. In between the games he looks at the photos around the room. There are only a few photos of the Cubs, but plenty of the Scouts mostly on camps. Mrs Colins asks him if he's interested in joining. He told her that he's tried, but Mrs D said no.

"I'll have a word with her and see if we can arrange something" she says.

"Thank you" he replies.

It's now time for the results of the fancy dress competition. One which Derek is totally unaware of, and yet he's called up as the winner, not by his name but as Mrs Mop. Mrs Collins nudges him to go onto the stage to receive his prize. He's happy he's actually won something for the first time, but he's now expected to walk on stage dressed in women's clothes to receive his prize in front of all those strangers. And those boys and girls aren't alone, their parents are with them. At least he was never called up by his name, that is at least a relief as he makes his way up onto the Wooden steps to the stage. The man presenting his prize is probably in his sixties chubby and smartly dressed,

"Well Done" he says,

Derek accepts his prize. A box of chocolates,

"What is your name" he asks,

Derek suddenly goes into mute mode.

"Err"

"Emm"

"Err"

He's not going to answer,

"ITS DEREK" shouts Mrs Colins

Derek's face immediately goes from shock to horror. His face bright red.

"Ooh, I thought you were a girl" the man says.

Dereks head goes down in shame even more so as the fat man thought he really was a girl. The party is called to end, and all are thanked for coming. Derek still standing there on the stage, head still down occasionally lifting his eyes to see if anyone's laughing, no-one is. Derek is just paranoid. He makes his way down the steps to Meet Mrs Colins who's waiting at the foot of the stairs.

"Congratulations, I knew you would win".

Though she didn't pre-warn him it was a competition, something that might have helped him prepare. Even he knew there's no way you can prepare to be embarrassed except not turn up.

"Thank you" he said.

There's just no way he could be upset with Mrs Colins. She's unique in her own way and would never deliberately set Derek up to be embarrassed, though he couldn't say the same for Mrs D, who came up with the idea of Mrs Mop. The question Derek never knew is, did she know it was a competition. He makes his way back to Redhouse walking as usual still again hoping he won't be recognised. This time with a box of chocolates grasped within his hand. As soon as he gets back there's no delay in him getting out of that dress and into his own clothes. With the box of chocolate in his hand, he heads straight into the playroom on the trampoline jumping as he eats the chocolates one by one, probably not the best thing to be doing, but an eleven-year-old has no sense of safety.

Chapter 44
Pantomime and Dares

It's early December, and the first signs of the cold winter comes as rain that's poured most of the day turns into sleet as Derek leaves school on Friday. He and the rest of the boys get home. As soon as they're changed they're straight into the dining room for tea which is unusually early. That's because they're going to a pantomime. As soon as Tea is over, the boys are instructed to get ready for going out. Darkness falls as they're ready to leave with a short walk up Shorthope Street to a waiting Coach. By now the sleet is falling as snow. As they sit in the coach, they're joined by a non-staff member. His only association with the home is supplying the ice cream. Derek instantly recognises him as the owner of Di Rollo the ice cream shop. The man takes his seat next to Derek.

"Hello" he says.

"Are you coming with us" Derek asks.

"Yes"

The coach sets off turning around at the roundabout a mile up the road after the racecourse. They both talk most of the way, though very little. They're heading into Edinburgh to the Kings Theatre for a pantomime. The pantomime is Jack and the Beanstalk with Stanley Baxter. Until that evening Derek had never heard of Stanley Baxter. But his performance is such Derek becomes a fan there on the spot. It's a laugh a minute when he takes to the stage, especially when he takes a shopping trolly in front of a large screen with a speeded-up film of a road. At the end of the performance he calls on the boys from the home as well as another group to stand. A bit embarrassing, but a night to remember. After the show, the coach returns with the boys walking back to Redhouse in the snow that forgot to settle resulting from the road being too wet from the earlier rain.

It's not the only time Derek ends up involved in a show. He himself along with his classmates would stand in front of the entire school in its production of "Joseph and his technicolour dream coat". Though for Derek this becomes a problem for two reasons. One, he struggles to read the words to learn the song. And two, as he tries to sing the song, he has a noticeable wave to his voice resulting in him being told just to mime it. Miming to the chorus was about the best he got as it's the only words that stuck in his head.

Christmas arrives and like with every other, the process is the same. The difference this year is the Christmas tree is much bigger than the previous years and therefore it is placed in the play hall. The rest is the same with bin liners full of toys. This time Derek gets a helicopter and jeep to go with the action man he got the previous year. And also a radio with changeable coloured covers, and like last year Christmas dinner is in the dining room, and again like last year, Derek stays up for the new year chimes.

January 1977, and the snow hits hard. On Saturday Derek as he's done almost every week for the past year, takes his shopping list to the butchers. Walking gently in the snow, along the untrodden freshly laid snowed pavement. Then turning into Kerr's wynd to the sight of a boy about thirteen/fourteen riding on his bike. It looks new, most likely his Christmas present. The snow had stopped in the morning but settled. The boy seeing Derek starts showing off riding up and down the little street. Attempting to do wheelies. Of course, even Derek knew it was inevitable that he would come off, and sure enough he does. Derek looks at him laughing expecting the boy much older than him to launch at him over his humiliation but he doesn't. He too realises how stupid he looks and laughs along with him. Derek carries on to get the meat from the butchers right around the corner. As he returns the boy on the bike has gone as he walks back along the road to Redhouse.

At school still with the snow, Derek is dared to take his tops off as the snow falls. He does, stripping down to his waist. It's cold, but he doesn't care. Not long after another craze takes hold. In the schoolboys toilets, the boys are dared to hold their breath with their thumb in their mouth while being pushed against the wall causing them to faint. Derek takes part in this only to chip his tooth as he falls flat on his face. With the exposed nerves, the pain becomes unbearable particularly when trying to breath in or eat and drink hot or cold. Something Derek would advise anyone not to do now.

As Dereks reaches his twelve birthday he's moved to the room next door. Haggis sleeps in the first bed by the emergency hatch. Derek is given the bed on the far-left side of the room. Haggis was always a bit of a rebel, though not in a bad way though depending on how you look at it. For the boys, he's the one who stood up for them. Though he himself probably doesn't know it. One night he sneaks a bottle of whiskey in and gives everyone a sip. Derek tries it, and finds it so bitter he never has another, but some of the others take a few more sips.

Shortly before the summer half term. It's breaktime and the school is out in the yard. Derek is playing with his mates running around the back towards the concrete boat which is the only object in the playground. As he runs past the huge wall that backs off from the houses one boy can be heard crying. There's crowd around him. Most of the kids are from Dereks class.

"what's happened".

He asks.

"Ewan has cut his leg on glass".

Derek pushes his way in and sees Ewan Slight with blood pouring from his lower leg sitting in the dirt with broken glass around him. Without any hesitation, he picks him up and carries him into the school accompanied by another child. Straight up the corridor to one of the offices, putting him down.

"Thank you".

The teacher said as Derek walks away making his way outside again. It's not till later he realises his clothes are covered in his blood. Ewan doesn't return after the half term as he's still recovering and is the last time Derek sees him.

Every week the class goes to Musselburgh grammar School for swimming lessons. They walk in pairs from the Burgh School to the grammar school where the pool is. The pool at the Grammar school is not only used for school swimming lessons. It's also used for recreational swimming on Saturday afternoons. A few of the boys including Derek are regulars. They reach the school gates as the grammar school kids are on one of their breaks. Just after entering the front gate, right there sitting on the wall in between two other boys is his worse nightmare. It's Joe, his hair now long but still as ugly. "If only his friends knew", Derek thinks to himself. Joe sees Derek and greets him with just two words.

"Fuck off".

No other comment. It's then Derek realises he been in Musselburgh all of this time. But "where" are his thoughts. Up till now he's enjoyed his freedom without the need to look over his shoulders fearing he might be following him, now realising that since he left Redhouse he could have had ample opportunities to attack his victims. They've reached the door to the swimming pool. After school he changes his ways making sure he's never on his own when possible. Back at the home that night he's distraught knowing he's out there in the same town wondering why he was never move away. They knew what he did. Why would they allow him to stay near his victims? So many questions but no one to answer them.

As the boys gather in the TV room in the evening for television before bed, a show of defiance comes in the form of Haggis. Mrs D orders him to get of a chair she wants to sit on.

"No, theres other chairs" he says

"I'm telling you to get off that one".

"No"

She grabs him trying to pull him off, but he fights it eventually standing up arguing with her. In the end he's sent out of the room. The other boys are slightly shaken by the altercation knowing Haggis is hotheaded and could easily take her down. He leaves the room possibly ending up getting a few blows from the strap, though it was becoming obvious the staff were probably more scared of him than he of them.

Chapter 45
Departure

It's late May and Derek gets a visit from Mr Black. They sit in the office.

"Derek, your dad wants to visit you".

"My Dad"

Derek says surprised by his words

"Yes, I've been calling him for some time now". Mr Black says

"When"

"This Friday"

"Oh, ok"

The discussion continues to go on for some time. Mr Black is explaining to him about his background and that his parents separated before he was born and he now has a stepmother, stepbrothers and sisters, and two real sisters, with no mention of Ann. Friday comes and Derek goes to school as normal. The celebrations for the Queens silver Jubilee have already began. Musselburgh along with other seaside towns are all historical fishing towns and most of the celebrations are centred around the Harbours. A temporary telephone was installed in Derek's classroom so Mrs Samuels doesn't need to leave the room, easing the strain on her heart condition. The call comes just before lunch.

"Derek you need to go home" Mrs Samuels says.

Derek gets up and leaves his books not aware that day would be his last day at school. He will never return on Monday morning, nor will he ever see his School mates apart from two. He leaves the room, runs downstairs, out the door, up the little steps by the gate he's ascended/descended since starting at the School leading to Mansfield road, then making his way down the footpath towards the Crossing on high street for the last time crossing the road then making his way to Redhouse. Both Mrs D and Miss Murray are at the front door waiting for him.

"This way"

Mrs D says enticing him through the garden gate. He goes into the hallway.

"Your dads on his way, and will be here any minute"

Derek is nervous and doesn't know what to expect. This is the first time in his life he'll meet a family member.

"Shall I change my clothes".

Derek asks, still in his school uniform.

"No, you'll be fine in those" Mrs D says

"What will you say to him when you meet him"

Miss Murray asks,

"A dinni ken" (I don't know)

His response as they wait in the office for his arrival. The yard gates are in clear sight from the office window. It's an anxious wait, then a car turns into the yard almost brand new.

"He's here" Mrs D says

They walk out the front door. A man emerges from the car. He's very dark skinned in a beige jacket wearing unmatched trousers.

"Go on" Mrs D says,

Derek looks up to them unsure about this. To him he's looking at a total stranger, his hair is curly, and he doesn't look anything like him. He takes a few steps forward, the man stands against his car smiling with his arms open. Derek is still reluctant to go to him.

"Go on its ok".

Miss Murray says trying to calm his nerves. He slowly walks over eventually reaching him. His dad wraps his arms around him. Derek keeps his arms down still not convinced this is his dad. He starts to speak but his English is broken. Derek looks back and both women are smiling as if they're watching a scene from "gone with the wind". But this is anything but a happy ending, or even an ending. Derek is still both confused and unsettled by this. He's never had a family before, and has never met this person standing in front of him or even seen a photo of him. He's just been told "he's your dad" and that's it. He feels no emotional bond towards him, or bond period. But it's a situation he has no control over realising he just needs to go with the flow. The man opens his car door and Derek again looks back. Mrs D waves the back of her hand signalling him to get in. He gets in. His dad starts the car and they set off. Dereks eyes are fixated on him. He's never been this close to anyone with such a dark complexion before. He drives up to the top of Mill hill then heads towards High Street.

"Have you eaten".

He asks in his strange accent.

"No"

"There's a cafe just down the road here, we'll stop there".

He says, as if he had already looked around the area. They stop at the café that's just across the road from the toy shop near the old Town hall. In they go. They sit near the window, his dad with his back to it and Derek opposite him facing the window. He picks the menu up glancing through it.

"Have you ever had Pizza" he asks.

"No"

"You'll love it, do you want to try it".

Derek nods his head with approval. He makes the order and while the order is being made, he starts telling him about himself and his family. How he would give his sisters anything they wanted and that they only have to ask. Derek still young is not fully understanding the magnitude of what's taking place right now, and how all of this will impact on his own judgement within the next 48 hours. He doesn't realise there's flaws in his statements. So far he's made no mention of his step brothers and step sister sisters. He just seems to concentrate solely on his real sisters. The pizza arrives and he takes a slice. It turns out he does like it. After lunch they head into Edinburgh sightseeing etc. They go on the beach where he finds out his dad can't run. Later they have a milkshake, another delicacy new to Derek. And another he seems to like. It's starting to get late and they head back. Once they're in the car he starts talking about his sisters again and how they can get beautiful dresses whenever they want them and money. They arrive back. Derek gets out of the car and heads back into the home.

"I'll pick you up tomorrow morning".

He shouts as he sets off back to his hotel. Miss Murray keen to know asks.

"How did it go".

"Ok"

"Is that it!"

"He talked a lot about my sisters".

"How many have you got".

"He says two".

He never named them thus Derek assuming one is Ann. He's completely forgotten that Mr black a week earlier told him about his family.

The next morning he turns up to pick him up. He's arranged to go to North Berwick for the day. As they drive out of Mill hill, he stops at his hotel which is opposite the racecourse. Both of them go in.

"Is this your son".

The lady at the reception asks, indicating he had spoken about Derek before.

"Yes"

They go upstairs to his room. It's small with two single beds. He opens his suite case and hands him a small bag of what looks like crisps.

"Here your sisters and your mother made this for you".

They only stay for a short time then leave making their way to North Berwick. They arrive to a bustling town with bunting everywhere. Its noticeable Whales bones high above the hill with the Queens silver jubilee in full swing. After parking up they make their way to the harbour. The trawlers have been turned into tourist boats for the weekend. Derek is excited, he spends a lot of time around Fisherrow Harbour but has never been on the boats.

"Can we go".

Derek asks his dad as he's watching people going on one boat with people coming off another. There are several boats out with some waiting to dock.

"I don't know, we'll have to see what it cost".

"It's free, look, it says it on that sign".

It's unmissable. The sign is big, but what Derek didn't know is his dad is looking for an excuse not to go on.

"I'll wait here, you go on".

Of course the sign says free in large print, but the smaller print says "children must be accompanied by an adult" neither have noticed it till Derek tries to get on,

"Who are you with".

The boatman asks,

"My dad"

"Where is he".

"Over there"

Pointing to him standing away from the harbour wall.

"You'll have to accompany him sir, he can't go on by himself".

The boat man shouts. His dad looks around. All eyes are on him,

"Ok"

He says making his way onto the boat knowing he has no choice now that the whole world has heard. They set off. They're not long out of the harbour when his dad starts feeling sick. With the waves hitting the boat and other boats passing causing the boat to go up and down he's finding it too much. Luckily the boat trips are short and run for about twenty minutes. As soon as their feet are back on steady ground the relief is noticeable, with Derek totally unaware he's about to rub it in asking,

"Can we have fish and chips".

"Let's walk around for a bit then we'll stop to eat".

His dad says, probably waiting for the contents of his stomach to settle before further intake. Throughout the day he continues to talk about his sisters, selling him the notion that whatever they want they get, then saying he too can have anything. The rest of the sibling come into the discussion as they head back to Redhouse. He's convinced Derek to return home with him with plenty of promises, also telling him,

"Don't trust anything they say if they try to stop you".

Derek is naive and not realising what that statement means but he agrees. That same evening Mr Black arrives to talk to Derek. They both go into the new Staff room. His dad has already told them he wants to take Derek home with him. Mr Black talks with Derek on his own.

"Is this what you really want".

"Yes"

"I would advise you to spend a week or two to see how things go".

Derek is still not fully understanding what Mr Black was trying to explain. More because he never came straight out with it. But perhaps he's trying to be cautious. Is this what his dad meant by not trusting anything they say, Derek wonders. It takes only a couple of months for Derek to understand the concerns of Mr Black.

"He treats me nice".

"Are you absolutely sure you want to go".

"Yes"

Mr Black pauses for a while before replying,

"Ok"

With that they leave the room. Mr Black heads towards the office whilst Derek heads outside.

The next day, Derek waits for his Dad to arrive. Mrs D walks into the TV room. Derek is on his own and the others are either in their rooms or outside.

"Derek, your dad's picking you up this afternoon. He wants to take you home today".

"Am I leaving".

"Yes"

Derek smiles but gets no response from Mrs D. He expected her to be happy for him but it's clearly not the case. It's a rare thing for her to be happy about anything, but he would have thought she would be happy for him going to his family. But even Derek realises something is not right.

"You need to start packing".

"Ok"

He makes his way up to his room, over to his bed and starts emptying his wardrobe and side cabinet. Everything is laid on his bed. Mrs D enters the room with a battered case. She opens it up placing it on the bed next to his and starts folding his clothes into a neat pile. Derek looks at her with almost shock. For him this is completely out of character. Is this the same woman that was mostly mean throughout his tenure at the home, something just didn't add up.

"It's best you leave your helicopter and jeep here. There's not much space to take it" she says.

Derek had already grown bored with it, so isn't too bothered.

"Ok"

"Right, I think we've got everything, let's go downstairs" she says.

As Derek reaches for the case, Mrs D beats him to it picking it up and heading towards the door. Derek takes one last look around the room locking his eyes onto the helicopter one last time before leaving the room. He walks behind Mrs D watching her quietly carrying his case downstairs. Both are silent, but Derek can't help but notice how out of character she is. He has no idea if she's sad or happy to see him go, or if she suddenly found her morals. But all he knows is this is not the Mrs D he knows. As they reach the first floor, Derek opens the room door and is about to walk the same route he's done two or three times a day since arriving.

"Come this way" she says.

Continuing to go down the last two flight of stairs. She takes his case into the office telling him to go into the TV room. A short time later the rest of the boys arrive in the room. Derek is presented with a gift, an Arsenal football kit, ironically giving he's still not into football. But to him it is a gift. He then joins them for lunch for the last time. After which his dad turns up. They pack the car. Derek gets in the front passenger side of the car. Looking up he sees the boys with their heads out the windows from both upper floors waving. He waves back. The car engine starts up and begins to move off. At this point, and for the first time in his life he feels deeply emotional. He turns his head facing the passenger side window. His eyes beginning to water up. It's becoming too much for him as tears start running with him desperately trying hard not to cry out. He feels the strain in his head, his nose is running, occasionally sniffing and wiping it with his sleeve. Not once looking towards his dad. It's finally hit him this maybe the last time he'll pass through the corridors of Redhouse. Walk the cobbled walls of the harbour walls. See his school mates and ride along the grove. He's now not sure if he made the right decision.

As they get to the end of Millhill he asks his dad with a broken voice to turn left.

"We haven't got much time". His dad says

"Please"

Derek replies pausing for a bit as he tries to compose himself.

"I have to see two people". He continues to say

"where" he asks.

"Just here, then over the roundabout"

"Ok but be quick we have to drive into Glasgow before we go home."

He stops just up the road. Derek gets out and runs across the road then up the steps to Lynda's house. He knocks on the door waiting for it to be answered. Her mum opens it.

"I'm leaving now". He says

She calls Lynda but she doesn't say much.

"Bye," she says.

"Bye," he replies.

He walks down the steps crosses the road then looks back. Lynda and her parents are at the door waving, he waves back before getting back into the car.

"We don't have time to go to the other house, we need to leave now," His dad says

With no reply from Derek, he turns the car around heading towards Glasgow. Derek never gets to say goodbye to Mrs Collins. A woman he always saw as a person who changed his thinking on life. A person who taught him the value of helping others.

For over an hour he continues to look out the window breaking into tears occasionally. Everything it turns out he was told by his dad was a lie.

Was his childhood any different when he moved? And yes, the character is the author with another different name. Why? Well, that's another story.

Printed in Great Britain
by Amazon